"YE SEARCH THE SCRIPTURES . . ."
— John 5.39

Ye Search
the Scriptures

WATCHMAN NEE

Christian Fellowship Publishers, Inc.
New York

Available from the Publishers at:

Box 58
Hollis, New York 11423

PRINTED IN U.S.A.

PREFACE

The Bible is the inspired word of God. Every child of His must know it by heart.

The Bible records the many things God did for us in the past and the many words He spoke. It also registers the many ways by which He led people in former days. It is therefore imperative for us to study the Scriptures if we would desire to know how richly and extensively God has provided for us.

The speaking of God *to* us today is based upon the words He has already spoken; His speaking *through* us today is also built upon what He has once before uttered. Hence we need to store the word of God richly in our heart before we can hear God's speaking today and before we can be used as ministers of His word.

The aim in our compiling this volume is to supply some prerequisites and principal methods of studying the Scriptures to those who have a heart to know the Bible. May God bless the readers as well as this book.

The Editor
Gospel Book Room
Shanghai, China

CONTENTS

The contents of this volume comprise a series of messages which were delivered in Chinese by the author during a training period for workers held in Kuling, Foochow, China, in 1948, and are now translated into English for the first time.

Scripture quotations are from the American Standard Version of the Bible (1901), unless otherwise indicated.

PART ONE

THE PREPARATION OF MAN

The Preparation of Man

To study the Bible well two basic conditions must be fulfilled: one, the person must be right and trained; and two, the method must be correct. For the past hundreds of years, especially those following the Reformation, scores of good books have been written on the subject of how to study the word of God. These have been volumes of high quality, yet they share a common defect of the first degree, which is, that they all emphasize the method of Bible study but overlook the person who studies the Bible. The authors give the impression that anyone can master the Scriptures if only he adopts certain methods. Yet the fact is that many have used these methods but still do not know the Bible. Doubtless, those who write about these methods know their Bible well. Why, then, do not people obtain the same result in following their methods? It is because they forget what kind of people they are. The problem of studying the Word lies not simply in method but most keenly in man himself. Some study well, for they have learned before God; consequently, by using the right method they are able to know the Bible. But merely passing on their method without simultaneously imparting their life will not help others whose life is not right.

One thing, then, is of supreme importance: in studying the Bible, the man as well as the method needs to be right. Indeed, only the right man may fully utilize the proper method. Study method is unquestionably quite significant; without it one cannot master his study. Yet the man himself must first be transformed before he is able to study well. Those who believe that only a few are able to understand the Bible are as mistaken in their thinking as are those who consider all as being qualified to know it. For the truth really is that neither few nor all but only one class of people may actually study the Bible. Unless we belong to this class of people we will not be able to study the Scriptures too well. We therefore ought to realize that the man stands ahead of the method. If the man is not right, not one method will work; but if he *is* right, all these good methods may be used. We sincerely regard method as necessary; yet we will never rank it first; *the man himself must be primary.*

Consequently, in approaching this matter of searching the Scriptures, we should naturally divide it into two parts: first, the preparation of man; second, the methods of Bible study. What now follows is the first part, with the second part to be considered later.

1 | Three Prerequisites

A. SPIRITUAL.

"The Words That I Have Spoken . . . Are Spirit"

The Lord Jesus once said: "The words that I have spoken unto you are spirit" (John 6.63). And hence the words of the Bible are not words only, nor are they mere letter, they are also spirit. We should not forget what our Lord has declared: "God is spirit: and they that worship him must worship in spirit" (John 4.24 margin). He is telling us there of a basic principle, which is, unless man exercises his spirit he is unable to touch God; for God being Spirit, we cannot worship Him except in the spirit. If we engage anything other than the spirit, we shall altogether fail to worship. We cannot worship Him with our mind, nor our emotion, nor our will. "Will-worship" (Col. 2.23) is of no value whatsoever. Because God is Spirit, He must be worshiped in spirit. This same fundamental principle governs in our Lord's later statement, recorded in John 6: "The words that I have spoken . . . are spirit." Since the Lord's words are spirit, they must be read in the spirit. In other words, spiritual things can be touched by the spirit alone.

This Bible which we have is more than words printed on paper. So far as its nature is concerned, it is spirit. Hence all who intend to read this book need to *use their spirit*. There is no other way to read it. Of course, the spirit we refer to here points to the spirit of the regenerated person. For the sake of convenience, let us for the time being call it "the regenerated spirit". Since not everyone has this regenerated spirit, neither can everyone understand the Bible. Only those who have this regenerated spirit are able to study the Scriptures. The spirit is to be used in reading the Bible as well as in worshiping God. Without this spirit none may know God nor know the Bible.

Perhaps you come from a Christian family. You may recall how before you were born again you may have read a great deal of the Bible, yet you could not understand a bit of it. You knew the histories in the Bible, you remembered the events recorded there, but you did not understand anything. This is not at all surprising, for the word of God is spirit. Unless a person uses his spirit he is unable to understand God's word.

When does man begin to understand the Bible? From the day he receives the Lord. Thereafter the Scriptures become a new book to him. He treasures it, and though he may not comprehend too much at the beginning, he loves to read it. Daily and yearly will he read it; he will sense hunger or loss if he does not. What is the reason for his understanding God's word in this way? The answer is in his being born again: "That which is born of the Spirit is spirit." The words of the Bible are spirit, and so too is the life which man receives at regeneration. It takes a man of the spirit to read the words of the Spirit. And only then will the Bible commence to shine and become effectual in his life. If a person is not regenerated, then no matter how clever and scholarly he may be, to him this book is a mystery. But a regenerated man whose cultural background may be quite primitive possesses greater understanding of the Bible than does an unregenerated college professor. And the explanation? One of them has a regenerated spirit, while the other has not. The Scriptures cannot be mastered through cleverness, research, or natural talent. The word of God is spirit, therefore it can only be known to whoever possesses a regenerated spirit. Since the *root* and the *nature* of the Bible are spiritual, how can anyone who lacks a regenerated spirit begin to understand it? It is a closed book to him.

"My flesh is meat indeed, and my blood is drink indeed," declared the Lord Jesus (John 6.55). When those unbelieving Jews heard this statement, they strove with one another, saying, "How can this man give us his flesh to eat?" Nevertheless, all who are born again know that this indicates He is the Son of God. We will bow down and confess, "My life comes from Your flesh and Your blood. Without Your flesh, I would have no life today. Without Your blood, I cannot even live today. You are indeed my food." In reading the Lord's word the regenerated will give thanks and praise instead of expressing puzzlement.

"It is the spirit that giveth life; the flesh profiteth nothing: the words that I have spoken unto you are spirit" (John 6.63). In these words of Jesus we see two realms: one is the spirit realm, the other is the flesh realm. In the spirit realm everything is living and useful; in the flesh realm, however, nothing is profitable. It is imperative that we read the Bible in the spirit. Regardless how learned a man is, or how resourceful in research, or how excellent in analytical power, he is not able to truly study the Bible if he lacks this spirit.

God is Spirit. Today we have the regenerated spirit, therefore we know Him. When unbelievers argue with us their eloquence may surpass us, their cleverness may exceed us, and their reasonings may seem more convincing; yet we know we know God because we have been born again—we possess the regenerated spirit by which we can touch God. It really does not matter whether we are able to explain or not; the reality is that we have touched God. Those who know not God hope to find Him through analysis, deduction, or reasoning. They may do all these, but still they cannot believe in God. For He is not to be found by human analysis and deduction.

"Canst thou by searching find out God?" challenges the book of Job (11.7). God is never arrived at through research. He is found by one way only—through the regenerated spirit. By exercising this spirit a person knows God through direct contact. Aside from this there is no other way. And the regenerated spirit is required in the study of the Bible just as it is needed in touching God. Suppose, for example, that a person desires to connect electricity to his installation. He has in his hand wood, bamboo and cloth, but no copper wire. Though the power company has an abundant storage of electricity, he has no way to make his electric bulbs shine. No amount of cloth, bamboo and wood can draw in the electricity. But there is another person who has neither cloth, nor bamboo, nor wood. All he has are some copper wires. But he is able to get his bulbs to shine because these wires of his will conduct the electricity. In like manner, man needs a regenerated spirit by which to touch the word of God as well as to touch God himself.

There is only one element in us which enables us to

read the Bible, and this is the regenerated spirit that we have. If we employ any other element to read the Word we shall not touch the things of God. The Bible is something that may become either flesh or spirit to us. In the case of a person who does not possess a regenerated spirit but has only the flesh and the things of the flesh, the Bible will become flesh to him; but in the case of another person who possesses a regenerated spirit, this spirit will operate in him so that in touching the word of God he touches the Spirit. This is not to imply that the Bible may change its nature to be unspiritual, for the word of God is spirit. Said Jesus: "It is the spirit that giveth life; the flesh profiteth nothing: the words that I have spoken unto you are spirit." His words are spirit. And to His believing disciples the words of the Lord were spirit, but to the unbelieving Jews they became flesh. To those who possess the regenerated spirit the words of the Lord are spirit, whereas to those who do not have this spirit they are flesh. The way many people handle the Bible is almost laughable, since they lack this regenerated spirit. Men should not read the word of God with their own mind and cleverness. What they need is this regenerated spirit.

"Interpreting Spiritual Things to Spiritual Men"

Why is it, some may ask, that though I am a regenerated person and possess a regenerated spirit I cannot read the Bible well? Why is this book closed to me? To answer this question we should read a passage in the Scriptures.

"And I, brethren, when I came unto you, came not with excellency of speech or of wisdom, proclaiming to you the testimony of God. For I determined not to know anything among you, save Jesus Christ, and him crucified.

And I was with you in weakness, and in fear, and in much trembling. And my speech and my preaching were not in persuasive words of wisdom, but in demonstration of the Spirit and of power" (1 Cor. 2.1-4). The subject of this 1 Corinthian chapter is concerned with Paul's preaching not in persuasive words of wisdom.

"That your faith should not stand in the wisdom of men, but in the power of God. We speak wisdom, however, among them that are fullgrown: yet a wisdom not of this world . . . We speak God's wisdom in a mystery, even the wisdom that hath been hidden, which God foreordained before the worlds unto our glory: . . . Things which eye saw not, and ear heard not, and which entered not into the heart of man, whatsoever things God prepared for them that love him. But unto us God revealed them through the Spirit: for the Spirit searcheth all things, yea, the deep things of God. For who among men knoweth the things of a man, save the spirit of the man, which is in him? even so the things of God none knoweth, save the Spirit of God. But we received, not the spirit of the world, but the spirit which is from God; that we might know the things that were freely given to us by God. Which things also we speak, not in words which man's wisdom teacheth, but which the Spirit teacheth; combining spiritual things with spiritual words" (vv.5-13).

The marginal note renders the last phrase above as "interpreting spiritual things to spiritual men". (Now in view of the context of this chapter, the marginal rendering seems to convey the better translation. Since in Chapter 3 the word "spiritual" has reference to men, the same word used near the end of Chapter 2 cannot mean otherwise. For to mean otherwise is not allowed by the law of interpretation.) Paul is here communicating spiritual things to spiritual men ("combining" in Greek may also be translated "communicating").

After reading this passage we can readily see the relation between the spirit and the Bible. Of course, Paul is here speaking of the words as revealed and taught by the Holy Spirit—the words of the wisdom of the Holy Spirit, not those of man's wisdom. What are the words according to the wisdom of man? Things which the eye sees, the ear hears, and the heart contemplates—these are man's words. But where does Paul's revelation come from? His revelation comes from the Holy Spirit, for He alone knows the things of God. How does man come to know this Holy Spirit revelation? Paul states that we must have the Spirit of God. This coincides exactly with what we have already seen in the Gospel of John. Who knows the things of God, save the Spirit of God? Without God's Spirit none can know these things. Paul therefore concludes that he speaks these things not in persuasive words which man's wisdom teaches but which the Holy Spirit teaches, communicating spiritual things to spiritual men.

Why does Paul limit the communication of spiritual things only to spiritual men? Because communication is impossible to some people. "Now the natural man receiveth not the things of the Spirit of God"; he is unable to comprehend spiritual things. "For they are foolishness unto him"; he would think that we who believe in the Lord Jesus are truly "crazy". "And he cannot know them, because they are spiritually judged" (v.14). The peak of this passage is reached at the words, "they are spiritually judged". Spiritual things can only be judged or discerned by the spiritual man; the natural man can neither judge nor know them. This is not a question of research. One may indeed spend time in doing research, yet he still is ignorant because he lacks a basic factor within him. The natural man is the soulical man. Scientifically, he may be called the psychological man; which means a man who is controlled by his soul. Speaking in spiritual terms, he is an unregenerated man. He is, like Adam, a living soul, void of God's Spirit, and therefore unable to know the things of God.

As a rule, after a person becomes a Christian he should know spiritual things. Yet why is it that many brothers and sisters still do not know? This is due to the fact that though they possess a regenerated spirit, they are not necessarily spiritual men. In 1 Corinthians 2 and 3 Paul lays stress on the "spiritual" rather than on the "spirit". John's emphasis is on "spirit" whereas Paul's is on "spiritual". Man needs not only to possess this spirit but needs also to be possessed by this spirit. It is absolutely necessary to have the spirit; there is no other way. But having the spirit he must live under its principle, walk according to the spirit, and be a spiritual man; otherwise it is still of no avail.

Let us illustrate this with a parable. Suppose you take to an orchard a man who is born blind. You try to tell him about a mango tree there and what the fruit looks like. Do you think the blind man can understand? Even should he be very clever, having an extremely sensitive hearing ability, he still will not be able to fully comprehend. He can never know the green color of which you speak. The world of sight is different from the world of sound, as it is different too from the world of thought. Even so, to know the spiritual world requires the exercise of the spirit. Not all who have eyes actually see, for only those who use their eyes may see. The blind, it is true, cannot see the mango; but neither can the person with sight see unless he uses his eyes. Neither the blind nor the seeing is able to hear the mango with the ears.

Our problem today is that whereas the blind do not have eyes to see the mango, the seeing try though unsuccessfully to hear the fruit with the ears. Just as the natural man is incapable of knowing God—for none can know God by his natural organ—so the regenerate cannot know God by using the same natural means. Not all who have the spirit know God. It is possible to have the Spirit of God in a person and he still not know God. If cleverness in the heathen does not render any help to the knowledge of God, can it ever be a help in a Christian? If mental knowledge cannot teach the heathen the Bible, can it ever instruct the Christian? The only way to know the Word is by using the spirit. The question is more than having a spirit; it is a question of using the spirit. None may infer that because he has a new spirit he is allowed to follow his old way instead of walking after the spirit. If the old way was unusable before he possessed a new spirit, it is equally unfit to be used today after he has obtained the spirit. The basic avenue to the knowledge of the Bible lies in the spirit. Hence in 1 Corinthians 2 Paul indicates that the question is not over having or not having the spirit, but over being spiritual or not being spiritual. Spiritual things can only be judged by spiritual men.

"And I, brethren, could not speak unto you as unto spiritual, but as unto carnal, as unto babes in Christ" (3.1). Here is another term, "carnal". The Corinthian believers are babes in Christ, since they are carnal. For this reason Paul adds: "I fed you with milk, not with meat" (v.2a). Not that they cannot touch spiritual things altogether, but that they can touch only the simplest revelation. Anything deeper is beyond their reach. Because they are carnal they can only drink milk; they cannot eat meat. Milk is consumed at the early stage of life; therefore it represents elementary revelation. But meat is used later in life; so that it points to higher and more advanced revelations. Only a small percentage of a lifetime is dependent on milk; yet some, like these Corinthian believers, seem unable to take in anything else for an inordinately long while. "For ye were not yet able to bear it: nay, not even now are ye able" (v.2b).

In 1 Corinthians 2 and 3 we are shown three classes of men: (1) *The natural man.* Such kind of man possesses merely what belongs to the soul. He may also be called the psychological man. A natural man is unregenerated, does not have the regenerated spirit, and lacks the faculty for knowing God's word. This class of people cannot understand the Bible at all.

(2) *The carnal man.* Such a class does indeed possess God's life, having the Spirit of God in them; but instead of walking after the Spirit they walk according to the flesh. Having the Spirit, yet not touching the Spirit; having the Spirit, yet not submitting to His authority; having the Spirit, yet not ruled by Him—this is the class of people that is termed the carnal men in the Bible. Their understanding of the Scriptures is very limited. They can only take in milk, not meat. Milk is food predigested by the mother, hence this reference of Paul's cannot point to direct revelation, it can only signify indirect revelation. Such people are unable to receive revelation directly from God. They are compelled to receive it indirectly from others.

(3) *The spiritual man.* This type of person not only has the Spirit of God within but also lives under the Spirit's power and walks according to the Spirit's principle. The revelation this class will receive is unlimited. The word of God states clearly that only the spiritual judges *all* things.

In this matter of studying the Bible, we must remember this basic prerequisite—that the man must be spiritual, he must follow the Spirit.

B. CONSECRATED.

Heart Must Be Open

The Bible is the word of God. It is full of God's light. This light is to enlighten all whose hearts are open to Him. "But we all, with unveiled face beholding as in a mirror the glory of the Lord" (2 Cor. 3.18). Beholding the Lord with unveiled face is a basic condition to being enlightened by glory. If anyone approaches the Lord with veiled face, how can he expect the glory of the Lord to shine on him? God's light shines only on those who are open to Him. Unless one is open to God, he has no way of obtaining His light. The problem lies in his being closed to God. His spirit, his heart, his will, and his mind are all closed to Him, and hence he will not have the light of the Bible to shine on him.

It is just like the sun which, being so full of light, is meant to enlighten the inhabited world; but if we sit in the house with all doors and windows shut, its light is not able to enter and shine upon us. The difficulty is not with the light, but with the person. Light can only illumine those who are open to it. Now if this is true in the case of physical light it is equally true with spiritual light. Whenever we close ourselves up, light is prevented from lightening us. Some believers are closed people to God, and they will therefore never see His light. Instead of only spending time on reading, let us also examine ourselves as to whether we are open to God. If our face is veiled, the glory of the Lord is unable to illumine us. If our heart is not open to God, how can He give us light?

Light has its precise law. It enlightens all who are open to it. The measure of openness determines the amount of illumination. Even if we should shut all doors and windows of a room, the physical light will still in some measure penetrate should there be any fissures. Consequently, it is not difficult to receive light. Simply follow this law of openness, and you will have light. Whereas, if this law of light is violated then there can be no light whatsoever. The one who is closed to God cannot be a person who knows the Bible, regardless how much research he engages in or how long he prays. It is extremely hard for anyone to expect enlightenment with a closed heart. God's light is not given unconditionally to man. For man to obtain God's light, he must fulfill its condition.

Although all the children of God have the same Bible, the enlightenment they receive from it varies greatly. Some seem to have no understanding of the Book at all, some receive a little light, while still others find it full of light. The reason for such variation lies in the readers. The light of God remains the same, but people themselves are not the same. Some are open to God, so they are able to understand the Bible; but others are closed to God, hence they are not able to understand. Some people's closure is complete, therefore their darkness is likewise total; while the closure of others is partial, and consequently the light they receive is partial. Whatever may be the degree of incapability to see—whether large or small, whole or partial—it all proves the darkness within us. Never think for a moment that to study the Bible well or not is an insignificant matter. If a person does not study the Bible well, it indicates one fact—this man lives in darkness! How very serious it is for a person not to be able to understand God's word and see the light therein.

The question may be asked, What exactly is meant by

being open to God? This openness must come from a consecration which is unconditional and without reservation. To be open to God is not a temporary attitude; it is a permanent characteristic before Him. It is not occasional, it is continuous. If one's consecration to God is perfect and absolute, his attitude towards God will naturally be unreserved and nowhere in him is he closed to God. Any indication of closure only points to the imperfection of one's consecration. All darkness comes from closure, and all closure comes from lack of consecration. Wherever consecration is lacking there is a place of reservation. Where one is unable to yield to God, there he must defend himself; and in that area he has no way to the truth of the Bible. For when he comes to that area, he will only circle around and around it. Simply stated, then, darkness arises out of closure, and closure stems from lack of consecration.

Eye Must Be Single

There are many places in the Bible which speak distinctively of the light. In Matthew 6 the Lord Jesus talks of the light of the heart: "The lamp of the body is the eye" (v.22). Notice how the Lord does not refer to the eye as the light of the body, but only as the lamp of the body. For light belongs to God, whereas a lamp belongs to us. Light is in the word of God, but the lamp is in us. Lamp is where we obtain the light. In other words, the lamp is where God puts His light and hence the place where we receive as well as release the light. In order to have God's word shine upon us it is necessary that we have the lamp in the body. Now this lamp is our eye, and "if therefore thine eye be single, thy whole body shall be full of light. But if thine eye be evil, thy whole body shall be full of darkness" (vv.22,23). To have our body full of light we are told by the Lord of one condition, which is, that our eye must be single.

What is meant by singleness of eye? Though we have two eyes, the focus is one; for both eyes look at the same thing simultaneously. Suppose a person has eye trouble. Instead of being single, the two eyes produce two foci, thus seeing two things concurrently though seeing neither clearly. For the eyes to see anything accurately there can be but one focus, never two. Now in order to receive light, the matter of whether the eyes can see or not is as much a problem as whether there is light. There will be no light if we have not received grace and mercy; but light is already in us if we have received grace and mercy. So our difficulty now is not concerned with light but with the eyes. If the eyes be evil, light will not be manifested. Unfortunately the eyes of many are not single; they see two things instead of one thing or see one thing as two things. As a consequence light is either dim in their lives or else they are totally in darkness.

"No man can serve two masters: for either he will hate the one, and love the other; or else he will hold to one, and despise the other" (v.24). The reason many cannot see light is because of their eyes being evil, which in turn is due to their lack of consecration before God. What is consecration? Consecration means: I will serve the Lord alone. A man cannot serve two masters. If he respects the one he will despise the other. If he hates the one he will love the other. It is absolutely impossible to serve two masters well. There is no way to strike a balance. No one can serve the Lord on the one hand and serve mammon on the other. Sooner or later he who serves two masters will encounter this dilemma. And he will finally come to love the one and hate the other. If a person does not consecrate himself fully to the Lord he will be serving mammon wholly. The Lord insists that the eyes need to be single, which means that our service and our consecration must be single. The singleness of a man's eyes expresses itself in the singleness of his service.

May God enable us to see this basic principle: that if we wish to study the Bible, to understand its teaching and to acquire the revelation therein, we have a responsibility before the Lord, which is, that we must consecrate ourselves absolutely and entirely to the Lord. Then shall we be able to see the light in the Scriptures. Whenever our consecration becomes doubtful, our vision becomes unclear. If our seeing becomes clouded our consecration must be faulty. Let us thoroughly learn that a man cannot serve two masters.

The other master is called mammon. What this term represents is riches or wealth. How the light of the Bible is impaired by mammon! Owing to the veil that is put on by mammon, many are not able to see the light in the Bible. They do not see the truth of the Word because they have this problem of mammon in them. They will not deny themselves the pursuit of wealth when they find the truth in conflict with their personal gain. If people could lay aside their personal gain or loss and pursue after the truth at whatever cost, they would quite naturally come to know the Bible. But due to the problem of mammon remaining unsolved, many have compromised the teaching of the Bible. Were Christians to have mammon fully dealt with, the number of those obeying God would be greatly increased.

For this reason, then, we need to take this warning to heart, for whenever we become careless and care somewhat for our own selfish gain, the light of God will immediately be veiled. In order to see light we must not serve mammon. We cannot have two interests—our own as well as God's. We can only consider one interest, which is God's. If we intrude our own interest we will instantly have two masters, and our eyes will not be single. The double-minded is unable to know the Bible; he who wishes to preserve his own interest is automatically disqualified. Only the single-eyed can truly study the Bible.

How can our eyes be single? "Where thy treasure is, there will thy heart be also" (v.21). This is quite singular: that if we are able to control mammon, we shall be helped instead of harmed by it. Our heart naturally loves mammon. It is quite difficult for us to incline our heart towards God and not towards gain. Yet if we could control our wealth, we would also control our heart. We should therefore learn to send out our treasure. For the Lord says here that "where thy treasure is, there will thy heart be also." When one dispatches his treasure to the Lord's side, his heart will just naturally gravitate to the Lord. By sending his treasure to heaven the believer sends his heart to heaven as well. Where our treasure is, there will be our heart. So by surrendering all to God our heart will spontaneously be all towards Him. And thus shall our eyes be single.

For us to understand the Bible we need to have a perfect consecration. How can our heart be inclined towards God if there is no consecration? Consecration produces a special action; that is, it sends our heart to God. When we consecrate our all to Him our heart cannot help but go to Him, because our treasure has already been dispatched there. Two different situations may happen at consecration: one person's heart may go first, whereas another person's heart may follow afterwards. Some are moved in their heart *before* they consecrate, while others consecrate and are then moved in their heart. Regardless what our heart condition may be, let us consecrate. Let us send forth the thing we are most reluctant to part with. In the name of the Lord, let it be dispatched to the needy. As we send it off, our heart will go to the Lord's side. When all things are sent to His side, our eyes spontaneously turn single.

As the eyes become single they begin to see clearly and are then able to be enlightened. "Thy whole body", says the Lord, "shall be full of light" (v.22). What is meant by having the whole body full of light? It means having sufficient light to teach our feet to walk, our hands to work, and our mind to think. In other words, we have light on all sides. Light will flood our emotion, our will, our mind, our love, our walk, and our way. No area about us remains unseen if our eyes are single.

We have already stated that only the spiritual can study the Bible. We will now add that only the consecrated can know the Bible. Except a person is consecrated, he will never be able to study the Word well. When he reads the Scriptures he will encounter this or that area where he has not yet consecrated, and darkness will be upon him. As he reads on, he will be confronted with more unconsecrated areas and more darkness. With darkness upon him, he is incapable of obtaining anything from God. And hence it behooves him to be absolute before God. He cannot serve the Lord on the one hand and expect to go his own way on the other. Someone may say: I really want to know the will of God, but I just do not know what the Bible teaches on this matter. That is his excuse; it is not true. He knows not because he has no desire to go the Lord's way. If he truly wishes to walk in the way of the Lord he shall see the path clearly marked out ahead of him. Only one kind of people is unclear—those whose eyes are not single.

Obedience Must Be Persistent

According to our obedience will God give the revelation of the truth of the Bible to us. The measure of our obedience before God determines the amount of light we receive. If we obey God persistently, we will see continuously. Without consecration, there can be no seeing; without persistent obedience, there will be no increase in seeing. Should our consecration be less absolute, our enlightenment will also be less complete; if our consecration is too general, our enlightenment cannot be any more specific. So that the basic problem lies in consecration. He who does not know consecration has no way to know the Bible. In order to see continuously, the consecrated must have not only that basic consecration once made but also a persistent obedience. The degree of enlightenment depends on one's obedience after consecration. To see fully demands perfect obedience.

Let us pay special attention to the word of the Lord Jesus: "If any man willeth to do his will, he shall know of the teaching, whether it is of God, or whether I speak from myself" (John 7.17). If any man wills to do the will of God, he shall know. In other words, obedience is the condition for knowing. *Willingness to do the will of God is the condition for knowing God's teaching.* It is completely impossible to know God's teaching without intending to do God's will. To know God's teaching requires the willingness to do His will. To will is a matter of attitude. God likes us to have this attitude of obedience. When it is present in us, God's teaching will become clear to us.

Instead of always asking what the Bible teaches, let us ask if we are willing to hear the word of the Lord. The problem lies with our attitude, not with the teaching of the Scriptures. Whether or not the Bible will become manifest hinges largely on our attitude, while God is responsible for His teaching. If our attitude is right God will immediately reveal His word to us. And another instant obedience with another right attitude, and we shall have another revelation of God. With right attitude comes revelation; with obedience to that revelation comes more right attitude and further revelation.

Many profess that they have seen the truths in the Bible, although those who will to do the will of God may alone truly see them. This "will[ing] to do the will of God" is the result of the persistent working of the Lord in us. Do not think that it costs nothing to see light. Each seeing is both precious and costly. Sometimes we have to be brought through severe experiences by God before we can see one single thing. God's light frequently comes to us by way of reflection; that is, it will shine on one area and be reflected on another area. Much of God's light is reflective in nature. By receiving light on this part, we are able to see light on the other part. More light here will assure us of more seeing there. If we are disobedient in one of the tests, we will soon lose the revelation. To see God's light clearly afterwards requires our viewing it from various directions. The more willing we are to pay the price on all occasions, the greater the light we shall be able to see. Our obedience will lead to another obedience, which in turn will bring in more obedience. One light will induce another light, and so it goes on. All God's orderings are purposeful. Whenever we miss two or three obediences, we invariably incur loss before Him.

Whenever and wherever we fail to see, it must be due

to some defect in consecration, irrespective of how much we believe ourselves to be consecrated and obedient. Failure to see can only be attributed to our defective eyes. God can never be lacking in light, but He may refuse to speak if He notices any unwillingness in us. He never coerces people, nor will He utter His words cheaply. The Holy Spirit seems to be very shy, for He withdraws the instant He finds any hesitation on our part. God will not give light to anyone whose consecration is defective. Therefore, failure to understand the Bible is not a small matter; it reveals a defect in one's consecration. Spiritual eye-salve needs to be purchased with price; it is not freely given. All seeings are costly; none is cheaply granted.

C. EXERCISED.

"Solid food is for fullgrown men, even those who by reason of use have their senses exercised to discern good and evil" (Heb. 5.14). "By reason of use" may also be translated "on account of habit" (Darby). In order to receive God's word one condition must be fulfilled. What is this condition? Solid food is for fullgrown men. Why is this so? Because they have developed the habit of consuming solid food. The fullgrown are able to take in solid food on account of the habit of having their senses exercised to discern good and evil. "Experience of the word of righteousness" in the preceding verse (v.13) means skillful in the word of God on account of habitual use. The word "use" or "habit" is an industrial term in Greek. It means "skillful". Among workers, some are new hands while some are skillful hands. The latter are those who have become skillful through a certain period of training. To be skillful in the word of righteousness means to be well trained in the word of God. For a person to understand God's word he needs to develop that skillful habit.

The Bible exposes its readers. Certain kinds of people read certain things out of the Scriptures. If you wish to ascertain a person's character and habit you need only ask him to read a chapter from the Bible and see what he gets out of it. A man of curiosity will read curious things out of the Bible. A man with a big brain will find the Bible full of reasons. A man who does not think will see only the letters in each verse. How true it is that a person's character and habit can be revealed in the way he reads the Scriptures. Now if these traits are not dealt with, they will lead the person astray and make his reading of the Bible fruitless.

What kind of character and habit is required for studying the Bible well?

(1) *Must not be subjective.* It is required of all readers of the Bible to be objective. No subjective person can study the Bible well, for he is not apt to learn. Speak to an objective person once and he understands. Speak to a subjective person thrice and he still does not understand. Many people do not hear and understand because they are too subjective, not because their brains are inferior. Since they live wholly in their own thoughts, they are unable to hear other people's words. Being already filled with their own opinion and ideas, how can they take in another's words? If they are thinking of water and people talk to them of hill, they will reckon it as the water of the hill. Can such people who fail to hear another's words hear the word of God? If they are not able to understand earthly things, how can they be expected to comprehend spiritual things?

One thing is rather surprising: all who know how to

read the Bible are very quick in hearing. You speak and they immediately understand. They fully comprehend what you have spoken. Not being subjective, they are able to read the Bible as well as to listen to others. On the other hand, to many other people you may speak once or twice, yet they get no impression at all. This is because they have too many things in them, too many thoughts, ideas and opinions. If we wish to test ourselves on subjectiveness, we need only observe whether we are able to understand people when they speak. Can we comprehend what they casually say? In view of the limited years we live on earth, our time will suffer a great loss if we are all the time subjective. The objective readers are ten times better than the subjective ones. For the latter may read the Bible ten times and still allow it to slip by without its leaving any lasting impression.

Recall the story of Samuel. When the Lord called him, he went to see Eli. He was a thoughtful lad. He reckoned that if anyone should summon him at night, it must be Eli. So when God called him, he thought it was Eli who did it. He must have heard Eli's voice countless times, yet why could he not distinguish this voice from Eli's? This was due to his subjectivity. His mind was already set on Eli who would call, and therefore he could not distinguish God's voice from Eli's voice.

The problem with some people lies in their not allowing God to tear down their subjectivity. No matter how they read the Bible, they get no impression. They seem never to be able to hear God's speaking. When we are reading the Word, our thought, our idea, our feeling, our heart—our all—needs to be open to God. In short, we must not be subjective. We shall increasingly see the importance of this principle. If anyone has not been dealt with in this respect, he is unable to study the Bible well.

But an objective person is waiting to hear God speak; there is in him a quietness which lets God speak. He who has arrived at such a position can easily understand what God is saying when he reads the Bible. The subjective person, though, cannot even tell what he has read, for spiritually he is hard of hearing—just as Hebrews 5.11 says: "Ye are become dull of hearing." He is so full of his own things that he has no room for the Word. Subjectivity is therefore a very serious matter. A subjective person has no way to hear God's word, nor is he able to touch spiritual things.

(2) *Must not be careless.* The Bible must not be read carelessly since it is a most accurate book, exact to its very last jot and tittle. The word of God will slip away through the least negligence. Just as a subjective person will miss God's word, so will a careless person lose its lesson too. Let us be careful. The more a person knows God's word, the more careful he becomes. To a thoughtless person, the Bible he reads turns casual. By listening to the way a brother reads the Bible, you can readily judge whether he is a careful or careless person. It is a very bad habit indeed to misread some important word or words in a verse or passage. Due to the bad habit of inaccuracy, we often are inexact in the knowledge of the Bible. How easily God's word may be taken in error if we are slightly careless.

Let us illustrate our point here. The Bible is very careful in its use of singular and plural numbers. The singular and the plural must be distinguished. For instance, the word "sin" has a difference in number in the original Greek. The singular number "sin" points to man's sinful nature, while the plural number "sins" points to man's sinful acts. Whenever the Bible speaks of God forgiving man's sins, it always has reference to man's sinful acts—plural in number. God never forgives man's sin in the singular number—that is, man's sinful nature. For sin in the singular number is not forgiven; nay, our sinful nature needs to be delivered, whereas our sinful acts must be forgiven. This is clearly distinguished in the Bible.

"Sin" and "law of sin" are also different. Unless a person is delivered from the law of sin, he is not delivered from sin. Romans 6 deals with the deliverance from sin, while Romans 7 speaks of the law of sin. If we are a little careless, we may think these two things are quite similar. When we come to Romans 6 we conclude that the problem of sin has now been solved, for does not Paul at the end of Romans 6 already connect it with the beginning of Romans 12 by raising the question of presenting the body and its members to God? Yet Paul knows something else very well: that to be delivered from sin requires the knowledge of "the law of sin"; and that to overcome "the law of sin" necessitates having "the law of the Spirit" mentioned in Romans 8. A careless person may deem "sin" and "law of sin" to be nearly alike; but then he will miss the word of God. For God's word is quite refined; every word of His has its emphasis. If we are not careful, we may consider God's word to be casual, and thereby fail to understand it.

Besides "the law of sin" there is another law in Romans 7, "the law of death". If we are careless, we may also take these two laws as being identical. In fact, however, they are totally different. Sin is related to uncleanness, whereas death is related to disability. "The good which I would I do not" is "the law of death", and "the evil which I would not that I practise" is "the law of sin". Doing what I would not do is sin, but not doing what I would do is death. Through co-death, we are set free from the law of sin; by co-resurrection, we are delivered from the law of death. Accordingly, Romans 7 shows us not only "the law of sin" but also "the law of death". If we are careless, these truths will surely be overlooked. One thing is evident: all who study the Bible well are careful and accurate people.

We may have been told that since we are now clothed with the righteous robe of the Lord Jesus—that is, that God has given us the righteousness of the Lord Jesus to be our righteous robe—we are no longer naked, thus enabling us to draw near to God. Nevertheless, there is no such teaching in the Bible. Nowhere do the Scriptures teach that God has given us the righteousness of the Lord Jesus to be our righteousness. It states instead that God has given us the Lord Jesus to be our righteousness. God has not torn a piece out of the righteousness of the Lord to be given to us as our righteousness, for *He has given the Lord Jesus himself to be our righteousness.* How vast is the difference here! The careless may consider the righteousness *of* the Lord Jesus and the Lord Jesus *as* righteousness to be the same, not realizing that the righteousness of the Lord Jesus belongs only to himself and cannot be imputed to us. Whoever comes to God must have righteousness. The Lord Jesus himself needs righteousness to come before God; His own righteousness is for His own use. And that righteousness is the righteousness which He lives out on earth. Now had it been possible for this righteousness to be transferred to us, we would indeed have had righteousness; but why, then, must the Lord Jesus die for us? But as a matter of fact, though, *His* righteousness cannot at all be transferred. It is forever His, and none can share in His righteousness.

What, then, *is* our righteousness? The Lord Jesus *himself*, and not His own righteousness, becomes our righteousness. With the exception of 2 Peter 1.1 ("the

righteousness of our God and the Saviour Jesus Christ"),
which carries a special meaning in it, all the other passages
in the entire New Testament speak of the *Lord Jesus
himself being our righteousness*, never His righteousness
becoming our righteousness. The righteousness of the
Lord Jesus qualified Him to be the Savior; since He has
righteousness, He has no need for personal atonement. He
himself is, however, justified by God and is given to us as
righteousness. We are clothed with Him. In being clothed
with Christ we are clothed with righteousness. We are
justified before God, not because we have so much good
work but because we are clothed with Christ who is our
righteousness. We are accepted in the Beloved Son, not in
the righteousness of the Beloved Son. In order to study the
Bible well, we need to be exact.

Some people suggest that it is the blood of the Lord
Jesus which gives us life, signifying that our new life is
based on His blood. They maintain that by drinking the
blood of the Lord Jesus we obtain life. What Scripture do
they use? They quote the word in Leviticus 17.14: "The
life of all flesh is the blood thereof." If we read these words
superficially we may view such interpretation to be
reasonable. Nevertheless, the blood does not give us new
life. *For the blood is for atonement; the blood is to satisfy
God's demand.* We find the ordained principle concerning
the blood in Exodus 12.13, which says, "When I see the
blood, I will pass over you." *The blood is for God to see.* It
is to satisfy His demand, not ours. There is only one place
in the Bible which speaks of the efficacy of the blood to
usward—that it is effective upon our conscience, which in
reality is Godward also.

What, then, is the meaning of "life" in Leviticus 17?
This word life is "soul" in the original language, and
therefore points to "soul life". The Lord Jesus poured

forth His own soul. Says Isaiah, "He poured out his soul unto death" (53.12). In shedding His blood the Lord Jesus poured out His soul. And this is for the sake of atonement. On the cross He cried with a loud voice, "Father, into thy hands I commend my spirit" (Luke 23.46); and having said this He died. His body was hung on the cross; his soul was poured out in the blood for atonement (man's characteristic is the soul; the soul that sins must die; hence the seat of man's personality must die); and His spirit was committed to God.

In John 6 are several references such as "He that eateth my flesh and drinketh my blood hath eternal life", and, "The bread which I will give is my flesh, for the life of the world"; but never once does it say that whoever drinks the blood has life. In order to obtain life there needs to be the eating of the flesh together with the drinking of the blood. Let us learn to be careful people. If we mix up what God has separated we can easily misunderstand His word. We must not read the Bible casually. By searching the Scriptures carefully, gathering the hundreds of passages concerning the blood, we may come to see that the blood is to satisfy God's demand, not ours.

Suppose someone tells us: We will not sin any more if the blood has cleansed our heart and washed away the root of our sin. How should we answer? We will reply: The blood of the Lord has never washed our heart. Nowhere does the Bible say that the blood of the Lord Jesus washes our heart. Instead, the Word indicates that God has given us a new heart. The heart is deceitful above all things; it cannot be washed clean. The blood is for atoning of sin, not for cleansing. It is for forgiveness, not for holiness (holiness before God and holiness in man are not the same).

Someone may raise an objection by saying, Does not

Hebrews 10 mention how the blood of the Lord Jesus washes our heart? No, the statement there reads, "Having our hearts sprinkled from an evil conscience" (v.22). Conscience is part of the heart; it is the only part where we are conscious of sin. The blood satisfies the demand of the conscience of our heart as well as the demand of God. As we realize how the Lord Jesus atones our sin, our conscience will naturally have no more consciousness of sin. So that the effect of the blood upon our conscience is not in keeping us from sinning but in freeing us from the consciousness of sin. Not to sin is the work of the Holy Spirit. We must not confuse the work of the blood with the work of the Holy Spirit.

We need to develop a habit of accuracy before God. If we are not accurate we will bring damage to God's exactness. People with the habit of inaccuracy will not be able to find anything from their reading of the Bible. We should understand that the Bible is so exact that it permits no vagueness. Let us accept the training for accuracy.

(3) *Must not be curious.* We should seek for accuracy, yet we must not be curious. The word of God is exact, but we are not to search it with a curious heart. If we do, we will miss its spiritual value. The Bible is a spiritual book, therefore it needs to be understood with the spirit. Should the intention of our search for its accuracy be the satisfaction of the urge of curiosity instead of the pursuit of spirituality, we have gone the wrong way. How pitiful it is that many look always for strange things in the Bible. For example, people spend much time trying to prove that the tree of the knowledge of good and evil is the vine. Such study of the Word is futile. Recognizing that it is a spiritual book, we need to touch life, spirit, and the Lord in it. By seeing spiritual things we see also the exactness of

its letter, because all things spiritual are accurate. We will go astray in our search if we do not approach it from the standpoint of seeking for spiritual things.

Some people travel along the path of inordinate curiosity, especially in the study of prophecy. They study prophecy not for the sake of awaiting the Lord's return but for the purpose of knowing the future. The difference between what is spiritual and what is unspiritual is tremendous. If we are only curious we will take all spiritual and precious matters and turn them into things unspiritual and dead. This is indeed most serious. We ought to discern before God what is valuable and what is not so valuable, what is essential and what is incidental. The same Lord Jesus who proclaims that "till heaven and earth pass away, one jot or one tittle shall in no wise pass away from the law" also declares that "ye . . . have left undone the weightier matters of the law" (Matt. 5.18, 23.23). The law is exact to the point that not one jot shall pass away, but it also contains what are deemed to be weightier matters. The inordinately curious choose the lighter matters for study. By traveling on the lighter road, they shall soon become frivolous. Their condition fits perfectly what the Lord Jesus meant when He said: "Ye . . . strain out the gnat, and swallow the camel" (Matt. 23.24). They strain out the least but swallow the most essential. Such way of studying the Bible is totally wrong; and it originates from our curious nature. How can we expect to study the Scriptures well if our nature remains untransformed?

These above-mentioned matters of subjectivity, carelessness, and curiosity are the common ills of man. We need to have these defects corrected before God so that we may become objective, accurate and incurious. Such traits are not formed in one or two days; they become habitual only after persistent self-discipline (or better said, Spirit-discipline). Whenever we take up the Scriptures to read, let us do so objectively, accurately, and incuriously. And when our nature and habit are duly corrected, we will then be able to study the Bible well.

2 | Three Penetrations

In order to study the Bible well we must also penetrate into three things of the Holy Spirit. Especially in the study of the New Testament, these three things are quite manifest.

First. The Holy Spirit desires us to enter into His thought. To understand the word of the Holy Spirit our thought must merge with the Holy Spirit's thought. This is particularly important in the understanding of the New Testament.

Second. The Holy Spirit inserts many basic facts within the Bible for us to enter into. If we fail to get into these facts we have no other way to know God's word. Particularly in the four Gospels and the Acts, the Holy Spirit wishes us to penetrate into those prevailing facts.

And third. The Holy Spirit wants us to enter into the spirit of what has been written. In many places we need to not only penetrate into the thought but into the spirit of that thought as well; not only the fact, but the spirit of that fact too. This is evident in the Gospels, the Acts, and the Epistles.

The above three things must be penetrated by each reader of the Bible. Who, then, but the instructed and the disciplined may enter in? Now because these three matters are still concerned with the problem of man—that of his being properly trained—we discuss them here rather than list them in the later section which deals with the methods of studying the Bible.

Let us see, then, how we can penetrate into these three things of the Holy Spirit.

A. ENTERING INTO THE THOUGHT OF THE HOLY SPIRIT.

When the Holy Spirit wrote the Bible He had in mind His own design and thought. A lesson for Scripture readers to learn is to touch the original intention of the Holy Spirit in writing such a passage, not merely to read the words or even to memorize them. The primary concern does not lie in seeking for an interpretation but in knowing what the original purpose of the Holy Spirit was in setting it down. It is well to remember that the value of a word rests not on the word itself but on the thought which it expresses. "Ye do err, not knowing the scriptures," answered the Lord Jesus Christ to the Sadducees (Matt. 22.29). These Sadducees had studied the word of God, yet they did not understand it. So while we are reading, we need to know where lies the intention of the Holy Spirit in saying such words. But in view of this, our thought must undergo proper dealings.

1. *Merge with the Holy Spirit's thought.*

A Bible student should be an objective person; he

ought not rely on his own thought. The Holy Spirit has a thought; man's thought needs to enter into His thought and to merge with it. As the Holy Spirit thinks, so I will think. It can be likened to a river, of which the Holy Spirit is the main stream while I am a tributary. The Holy Spirit is like a big stream, I am like a small streamlet. The water of the streamlet and the water of the stream merge and flow together. If the stream flows eastward, the streamlet also flows eastward. In spite of the smallness of the streamlet, it will reach the vast ocean if it flows with the big stream.

The emphases in the Bibly vary: sometimes it stresses on the fact, sometimes on the spirit, but sometimes on the thought. Whatever the emphasis may be, all three elements are always present. In the instance where thought is foremost, there will also be present the spirit and the fact, and so on and so forth. Now when we encounter the thought of the Holy Spirit, we must be so objective as to be able to follow His thought. This is found to be impossible with some people. They may force themselves to think after the Holy Spirit for ten minutes, but then their own thought automatically takes over. Such subjective persons are unable to study the Bible. The dealing of the person is therefore one of the basic conditions for studying the word of God.

While reading the Scriptures one needs to use his mind; but his thought and the Holy Spirit's thought must proceed along the same line and in the same direction. Wherever the Holy Spirit goes, there I go. Find out what the trend of His thought is in this book, chapter, passage or sentence. Follow Him with singleness of mind. Discover what the Holy Spirit says, what He thinks, what His main thought is; and also what is but His side thought. In reading a passage of the Bible the first question to be asked should be: What was the original intention of the Holy Spirit in writing such a passage? If we are ignorant of the Holy Spirit's intention, we may in the future wrongly quote the Scripture. It is not enough just to read the letter of the Bible, memorizing it and knowing some fragmentary meanings about it. To study the Bible is to study the thoughts of the Holy Spirit through Paul, Peter, John, and others as they speak or write. And the understanding comes only when man's thought and the Holy Spirit's thought merge into one.

There was a story about a believer who purposely traveled from Egypt to Palestine by following the forty-two stations which the children of Israel had once traveled. He turned around wherever they had deviated. By closely following this course, he finally arrived at Palestine. Later he wrote a book telling about the way he journeyed. His course was not decided by himself, he was only following the footsteps of Moses. This is exactly how we should study the Bible: we should not decide our own course; we must instead follow the Holy Spirit. When Paul goes to Jerusalem we too go to Jerusalem. Whatever might be his feeling and thought, we too feel and think the same way. We ought not have an independent course; we should follow the course set by the writers of the Bible, even following the course of the Holy Spirit. The current readers must think what the past writers thought. The Bible readers must be moved by the Holy Spirit to think on the same frequency as were the writers of the Bible moved to think. Should our thought be able to follow the Holy Spirit's original thought, we will understand what the Bible says.

2. *Find the stem and the branch.*
     The word in the Bible has its theme as well as its

explanation. Some words are of primary significance, others are of a subordinate kind. Some are like stems while others are like branches. We should not pursue the branches and abandon the stems, nor should we notice the stems and neglect the branches. We need to observe carefully what the Holy Spirit is aiming at in each particular book; how does He say it, how many things does He mention, and with how many words does He finally reach the goal. Let us follow the thought of the Holy Spirit and think about these things step by step. Keep in mind that the Holy Spirit has His main thought as well as His explanation. Just as someone, for example, puts in a few words of explanation after he has begun to write some topic. This could be called the branch. A branch, though, never grows to heaven without returning to earth. Hence after the Holy Spirit has explained with five or ten verses, He will come back to the stem. Let us not be so occupied with the explanation that we fail to return to the main subject if the Holy Spirit leads. In the Epistles we frequently find a passage of main thought being interpolated by a section of explanation. In order to understand what we are reading we should clearly distinguish what words are stems and what words are branches. We must not simply rush through. When the Holy Spirit diverts to explain, let us also turn aside. When He returns to the theme, let us too return to the theme. If we desire to follow the Holy Spirit's thought, we have to be very responsible, neither trusting in ourselves nor having any confidence in the flesh.

The word in the Bible has its stems and branches, and these two are mutually joined to form a complete whole. For instance, in writing the Letter to the Romans the Holy Spirit did not give us some isolated verses such as 3.23 or 6.23 or 8.1. The entire book presents a full thought, a complete entity, not lacking in anything. For this reason, we must not preach on some verses that are taken out of their context. We may borrow them for specific reasons, but we need to make a distinction between borrowing from, and expounding, the Scriptures. Even in borrowing, we still must understand the context lest we misuse them as a pretext.

Once having had our thought disciplined, we will now be able to learn how to *fix the light* with our thought. Light shines for but an instant; it therefore needs to be fixed by thought. If our thought be undisciplined, not knowing how to enter into the thought of the Holy Spirit, we will be unable to fix the light with thought when revelation comes. Consequently, our thought must be so disciplined as to be totally objective and fully following the Holy Spirit.

The Holy Spirit has His way of speaking. For example, Romans Chapters 1 and 2 speak of man's sin; Chapter 3, of redemption; Chapter 4, of faith; Chapter 5, of the sinner; Chapter 6, of the sinner who died; Chapter 7, of the two laws; Chapter 8, of the Holy Spirit; Chapters 9-11, of that which are illustrations; Chapter 12, of Christ and the church; and Chapters 13-16, of the various facets of conduct of a saved person. When we read this book, we need to know what the Holy Spirit intended to say at that time. Let us notice that in each section of this letter the Holy Spirit has His primary thought. He first speaks of man's sin, then on its solution and the realization of the righteousness of God. This is followed by the matter of faith and the difficulty with faith which is man's work. Besides the problem of man's sin there is also the problem of man himself. So that in Chapter 6 the Holy Spirit dwells on the sinner (or old man) crucified. The problem of man's sin is solved by believing in the Lord as our substitute; the problem of the sinner is solved by believing in co-death with the Lord. In Chapters 9-11 the Spirit uses Israel to illustrate the grace of God and faith. Then in Chapter 12 He describes the situation of a consecrated Christian; and so forth. From Chapter 1 through Chapter 16 Paul's inward feelings are quite noticeable. And these are the stems. But as to the branches, even within the first section there are some. When the Holy Spirit is explaining man's sin He singles out the Jews as well as the Gentiles before He returns to His main thought. In the study of the Bible, therefore, we must follow the thought of the Holy Spirit.

3. *Two training methods.*

In order to train our thought we may adopt either of the following two methods.

First method—Separate the text and the explanation. In searching the New Testament we may try to put all the Holy Spirit's explanations within brackets. All in brackets are branches, while those outside the brackets are stems. By going through the "bracketless" material we may quickly discover the main thought.

Let us try this method in Romans. "Paul, a servant of Jesus Christ, called to be an apostle, separated unto the gospel of God" (1.1). This is distinctly the introductory word to the book of Romans. "Which he promised afore through his prophets in the holy scriptures, concerning his Son, who was born of the seed of David according to the flesh, who was declared to be the Son of God with power, according to the spirit of holiness, by the resurrection from the dead; even Jesus Christ our Lord" (1.2-4). This is to explain the gospel; and hence it is the branch. We may put these three verses in brackets. "Through whom we received grace and apostleship, unto obedience of faith among all the nations, for his name's sake" (1.5). This is

the text. If we study the entire book of Romans in such a
way we may be able to see the main thought in this letter.

At the outset do not go for the explanation. Separate
out the text first and then study the explanation. Find out
the main thought of the Holy Spirit and add to it the
explanation afterwards. What is the gospel? "Which he
[God] promised afore through his prophets in the holy
scriptures." God first prophesies of the gospel before He
sends the Lord Jesus to realize it. In the realization of the
gospel there are two parts: that of the flesh and that of the
spirit: one is the life of the Son of Mary on earth and the
other is the life of the Son of God in heaven. The four
Gospels dwell on the fleshly part, while the Epistles speak
of the spiritual part. So when we read, we may connect
verse 5 with verse 1, leaving verses 2-4 for later study.
Always read the main thought first and then read the
explanation; and in this way we shall enter into the
original thinking of the apostle. The whole Bible, especially the Epistles, should be read in this manner. Every
servant of God must know what is the main thought or
theme of each book and what is its explanation. This is the
first step to take.

What is the advantage of taking this first step? It helps
us to see in a certain passage how many are the principal
truths and how many are their explanations. When we
stand up to be ministers of God's word we ought to give
main thoughts together with explanations. Although as
ministers of the Word we will never be able to equal the
early apostles in their perfection and depth, the same
principle nonetheless governs us all. As soon as we
separate the text in the Scripture from its explanation, we
immediately observe a most wonderful fact, which is, that
the amount and degree of explanation given in the Bible is
exactly right. We will bow down and worship the Lord,

saying, How perfect is Your word! In delivering a message, how easily our words become weak and elementary by using too much explanation and illustration. Let us notice the way explanation is given in the Bible. Words of explanation should not be used profusely; explain only when people do not understand. Explanation is to make people understand, hence it ought not be used too much. How well balanced is the way the Holy Scriptures are written.

Second method—Let us try to rewrite the text with our own words; paraphrase it with words which we ourselves consider as easily understandable. For example, Romans 1.1,5 and 6 are the text. These words are written by Paul. Now after we have comprehended the thought of Paul, let us try to set it down in our own words. Start with rewriting only the text, not the bracketed explanation. This resembles the writing down in our own words any story which is related to us by our teacher after we have understood it. In paraphrasing the Scriptures we must be as objective as possible, that is, rewriting passages in accordance with their original meaning without adding our own thought. We need to train ourselves to be such as follow the thought of the Holy Spirit, merging our thought with His.

No doubt we may make mistakes in paraphrasing the Scriptures. After several times of correction, though, we can one day be more accurate in such work. Should a person be willing to learn in this manner, he will more easily understand the Lord's word. What is essential is to set ourselves completely aside. We will fail if we are either proud or subjective. We must learn to be objective, humble and meek. The thought of the humble and meek will naturally follow the thought of the Holy Spirit. Each one who studies the Bible should learn this lesson.

B. ENTERING INTO THE FACT OF THE HOLY SPIRIT.

1. *Factual impression.*

The second item which the Holy Spirit demands in us while we read the Bible is having factual impression. The Bible is not all doctrine, since many of its parts deal with facts, histories, and stories. The Holy Spirit, through these facts and histories and stories, expects to produce some impression in us, it being quite easy for Him in this way to speak the word of God to us. If the word of God fails to create an impression, it will slip by us without leaving any anticipated effect.

The impression mentioned here refers not to familiarity with whatever story there be but to a definite image that emerges out of the characteristic of the story. Each event as recorded in the Bible has its characteristic. If we fail to recognize this special feature we will not be able to understand God's word. It can be likened to a contract which is effective not with just any seal affixed, but only with the right seal. Hence the impression here discussed stresses more on the characteristic than on the contents of any event. In discovering its characteristic we may be able to hear what God especially desires to say at that particular juncture. It is possible to remember a thing, even to relate that thing, and yet miss its distinctiveness, thus failing to understand God's word. In the New Testament are found the Epistles and Revelation as well as the four Gospels and the Acts. While we read the Epistles we need to enter into the Holy Spirit's thoughts; as we read the four Gospels and the Acts, we need to have a heart which the Holy Spirit is able to impress upon with facts, causing us to sense the difference between this and the other facts, thereby knowing the distinctiveness of each fact.

To be impressed with an impression is like taking a picture. Several decades ago a square inch of film was overlaid with tens of thousands of tiny particles of silver bromide, so that the picture reproduced was not too attractive due to these dark spots. Later on, a great improvement occurred in which there was no longer any dark spot in the picture. Since an inch of film was now covered with several millions of silver bromide particles the impression became clear and distinct. In like manner, the more delicate and sensitive we are within, the more and clearer the impressions we receive; but the less refined we are within, the less impressions we obtain. If a person's heart and spirit are open to God his sensitivity will be developed to such a high degree that whenever the fact of the Holy Spirit passes near him the impression he receives will be sharp and deep. A spiritually delicate and sensitive person will at least see two things: first, he will naturally notice the emphasis which God wishes to reveal in His word; and second, he can detect the difference between what God intends to speak in one particular fact from what He intends to speak in the rest.

All who are spiritually dull fail to appreciate the fineness of the word of God. For God's word to leave within them an indelible impression, they must be inwardly meek and exceedingly sensitive. Thus shall they grasp the fine points as well as the sketch of the word.

2. *Delicate feeling.*

Many desire to see the fineness of God's word, but due to their lack of delicate feeling they fail to catch these exquisite points. Let us test this out on the four Gospels and the Acts which all narrate things concerning the Lord Jesus. These five books give more of the facts about the Lord Jesus than do the Epistles. We ought to acquire exquisite impressions from these facts. Let us illustrate with the following examples.

a. *By Way of Contrast*

Example 1
Zacchaeus and the Two Disciples at Emmaus

As we read Luke 19 and Luke 24 we notice that the facts concerning the Lord's coming to Zacchaeus' house and His coming to the house of the two disciples at Emmaus were totally different. To the house of Zacchaeus the Lord himself wished to go, but at Emmaus He made as though He would go farther. Whoever is sensitive sees at once that the Lord Jesus had done two entirely opposite things. In the one case the Lord was helping a sinner, despised by all—for Zacchaeus was not just an ordinary tax-collector, he was a chief collector. Without waiting for his invitation, the Lord Jesus voluntarily expressed the desire to go to his house. Zacchaeus himself had actually wanted to see the Lord, yet he dared not address Him, being shameful of his infamy as well as realizing his small stature. In such circumstances as these, it was the Lord who offered to come instead, saying: "Zacchaeus, make haste, and come down; for today I must abide in thy house." With respect to the sinner who really sought Him and yet dared not come to Him Jesus invited himself to Zacchaeus' house. The Lord knew the tax-collector's heart. How very delicate, therefore, was the Lord's feeling. And if *our* inward feeling is delicate, we too will understand.

The two men of Emmaus, by contrast, were backsliding disciples. Their eyes having grown dim spiritually, they failed to recognize the Lord when they met Him. The Lord walked with them and talked to them, explaining the Scriptures. When the two men approached the village where they were going, the Lord Jesus appeared to be going farther. His attitude towards these two disciples was quite different from his attitude toward Zacchaeus. To the latter the Lord was meek to the extent of voluntarily offering to stay in his house because He knew how great was Zacchaeus' outside difficulty and how unutterable was Zacchaeus' inward suffering. But these two men of Emmaus once knew the Lord. Yet they were now backslidden. And even after hearing many words from the Lord, they still proceeded to Emmaus. Hence the Lord appeared to go farther until they constrained Him to stay. In the one case a man faced towards the Lord, while in the other case two men backed away from the Lord. This is why the Lord's attitude towards them was different in each case. If we can touch the delicate feeling of the Lord Jesus we will then be able to reach Jesus of Nazareth whom God desires to reveal to us.

Example 2
Peter's Two Times Fishing

In Luke 5 it is recorded that Peter fished the whole night through and got nothing. But when the Lord Jesus said to him, "Put out into the deep, and let down your nets for a draught," the fishermen obeyed and enclosed a great multitude of fishes. Formerly they had caught nothing; now, strangely, they enclosed a great multitude of fishes. This moved Peter to fall down at Jesus' knees, saying, "Depart from me; for I am a sinful man, O Lord." Again, in the record of John 21, Peter went fishing. The Lord asked them, "Children, have ye aught to eat?" To which they answered "No". So He once again said to them,

"Cast the net on the right side of the boat." They did so and drew up many fishes. In the first fishing incident the Lord revealed His glory to Peter, a glory so transcendent that under its enlightening Peter saw how sinful a man he was and how unworthy he was of the presence of the Lord. But in the second fishing incident, which happened after the resurrection of the Lord, the moment Peter knew it was the Lord he jumped into the sea and swam to the shore. It looked as though, once he recognized the Lord, Peter wanted the fishes no more. The same revelation produced two different results. In the first instance it caused one who had never known himself to know himself, thus asking the Lord to depart from him; whereas in the second instance it drew one who had already known the Lord to come even closer to Him. And thus we should have different impressions from these two different facts.

Example 3
The Lord Multiplying Bread and
Mary Anointing the Lord

Two incidents are recorded in all four Gospels: one is the Lord multiplying bread to feed the five thousand, and the other is Mary anointing the Lord with nard. After the Lord had multiplied the bread and fed the five thousand He ordered His disciples to gather up the broken pieces which remained over, that nothing be lost (John 6.12). This is rather unusual, for the Lord had been willing to multiply the bread yet he ordered that the remaining broken pieces be saved so that nothing be wasted. Later on, when the disciples complained about the woman who had broken her cruse and had poured pure nard on the Lord (saying, "To what purpose hath this waste of the ointment been made?"), He replied, "She hath wrought a good work on me" (Mark 14.3-9).

Here we find a contrast between the multiplying of bread and the anointing with nard. In the one event there should be nothing wasted; in the other, that which appeared to have been wasted was not at all considered wasted. What was the result of a miracle ought not to be wasted but what was bought with three hundred shillings was not at all wasted when it was poured on the Lord. That pure nard bought with three hundred shillings was not given to the five thousand to use, it was given to the Lord to consume. That nard should not be gathered up, but instead the cruse containing it must be broken. It was not twelve baskets, it was one alabaster cruse. These are contrasts. The Son of God collected the broken pieces of the bread multiplied miraculously, yet He accepted the consecration of the nard worth three hundred shillings without reckoning it as extravagant. All four Gospels record this incident. And whensoever the gospel shall be preached throughout the world, said the Lord, that also which this woman has done shall be spoken of as a memorial of her. As widespread as is the gospel, so too is the message of consecration. Wherever the gospel is proclaimed, the dedication to the Lord follows. Now we must have just such an impression as this within us.

Example 4
The Lord under Judgment and
Paul under Judgment

It sometimes is very instructive to compare the four Gospels and the Acts. For instance, notice that both the Lord Jesus and Paul were under judgment. When Paul was being judged he declared he was a Pharisee, and a son of Pharisees (Acts 23.6). This was quite different from what the Lord Jesus affirmed when He was under judgment. Although we treasure our brother Paul, the best the earth can produce is but a son of man, whereas Jesus of Nazareth is God's only begotten Son. By comparing them, we notice right away that one is God's only begotten Son while the other is but a child born of God; one is the Lord while the other is a servant; one is the teacher while the other is a disciple. In spite of the fact that Paul has reached quite high spiritually, he can never be superiorly compared with his Lord. How delicate needs to be our inward sense, if we are to know the apostles in the Acts and to know the Lord in the Gospels. If we are less sensitive we shall not be able to fully receive the impression the Lord would wish us to have, thus preventing us from falling down before the Lord and worshiping Him. A careless person will read the Bible as though reading an ordinary story; the Holy Spirit is unable to give him the proper image.

Example 5
The Lord's Passing Through and Paul's Being Let Down

Once the Lord Jesus was in the synagogue in Nazareth. After the Lord had read from the Scriptures and had spoken for a while, He was brought by a mob to the brow of the hill that He might be thrown down headlong. But He, passing through the midst of them, went His way (see Luke 4.29-30). How very dignified was the scene! Yet how different this was from Paul's experience of being lowered in a basket down over the wall (see Acts 9.25). This is in no way suggesting that Paul was not right; it simply implies that he was inferior in quality to Christ. The Lord just passed through the midst of the people. What an impression this gives to us! When the Lord passed through the midst of those who desired to hurt Him, those people could only glare at Him stunned. How honorable and glorious is our Lord.

b. *By Way of Similarity*

To obtain proper impressions to be derived from the Bible it sometimes requires a contrast such as the five examples just mentioned indicate; but sometimes it needs similarity as well, that is, a joining together of similar cases in order to obtain a chain of impressions.

(1) People's Complaints against the Lord

Case 1
The Lord Asleep in a Boat

It is recorded in Matthew 8.23-27 that on one occasion the Lord Jesus crossed the sea with His disciples. Suddenly there arose a great tempest in the sea, but the Lord was asleep. His disciples were panic-stricken and awoke Him, saying, "Save, Lord; we perish." Mark 4 adds this to it: "Carest thou not?", as though to indicate: How could you still be asleep? In saying such things the disciples were expressing their complaint against the Lord. They not only cried out for help, they also registered their discontent. Whereupon the Lord Jesus got up, rebuked the wind and the sea, and there was a great calm. But He then turned around and chided them for their little faith. Now the Lord had His reason for chiding them, because He had only just told them: "Let us go over unto the other side"

(Mark 4.35). If *He* said over to the other side, they would most assuredly reach the other side. What, therefore, had they to fear on the way—be it tempest or waves or any other thing? The Lord Jesus was teaching them the lesson of faith. What is faith? Believing in what the Lord has said; namely, "go over to the other side." It is absolutely impossible for the boat to sink to the bottom of the sea after the Lord has said: Over to the other side. This then was the reason the Lord chided them, because they had not believed.

A most amazing fact is that the Lord Jesus never apologizes to any man. Usually the more instructed a person is before God, the more apologies he will make. He who has learned more is much more sensitive to the feeling of others, and therefore he invariably will apologize more. But the Lord Jesus is exceptional—He never apologizes to anyone. At first glance the disciples seemed to be right and the Lord Jesus wrong in this incident. The storm was raging and the waves were beating upon the boat. "Carest thou not that we perish?" Even so, when the Lord Jesus got up He made no apology. His not apologizing is His glory. He knew He had not overslept; He had done no wrong. He had said: "Go over to the other side"—and they would indeed go over to the other side! No one can uncover any word spoken by the Lord which is empty and void: none can face Him to fault Him on any point. This proves how glorious is the Lord!

Case 2
Woman with Issue of Blood Who Touched the Lord

The same principle is seen in the case of the woman with an issue of blood touching the Lord, as recorded in Mark 5. When that woman touched Him, the Lord

wheeled around and asked, "Who touched my garments?"
His disciples said to Him, "Thou seest the multitude
thronging thee, and sayest thou, Who touched me?" Their
tone revealed their discontent with the Lord. But the Lord
did not say, "Sorry, I have asked wrongly." Instead, He
looked intently round about to see her who had done this
thing. What He had really meant by His question was:
Someone has touched Me, and yet you did not know. You
notice only those who throng, but I note the one who
touches. Judging by appearance, the Lord seemed to be
wrong and the complaint of the disciples seemed to be
right; but in actuality the fault was with the disciples and
not with the Lord. Never once does our Lord apologize to
anyone. How exceedingly glorious is this fact which
should cause our hearts to bow down and worship.

Case 3
Lazarus Died

Once more, as told in John 11, people complained
against the Lord. "Lord," said Martha, "if thou hadst been
here, my brother had not died." She was blaming the Lord
for His late arrival. Had she not sent messengers to Him
days before, and why then should He come so late? And
because He had indeed arrived so late, her brother had
died and had even been buried. "If thou hadst been here"
gave vent to the deep resentment in Martha's heart. In our
viewing the scene outwardly, Martha's word seems to be
so justified. Nevertheless, the Lord understood perfectly
whatever He was doing. He purposely delayed coming for
two days in the place where He was. Men could consider it
too late, but the Lord Jesus delayed with purpose. Our
Lord never apologizes, because he is never wrong. We
apologize, for we have fault; indeed, if we never apologize,

we are really too proud. The more meek and humble we are, the quicker we will apologize. Not so with the Lord. Though He is humble and gentle, He has nothing to apologize for, since He has never done wrong. When people express their discontent with Him, He has not the slightest sense that He is wrong. He knows exactly what He is about.

There are many similar cases in the New Testament like these. Let us here learn a principle: that whenever we find similar situations in the Bible, gather them all together. From the three cases above we can discern a most glorious fact, which is, that throughout His entire life our Lord has never taken back a word or retraced a step. How beautiful and glorious is this fact! Which is more glorious—the healing of Lazarus or the raising of Lazarus from the dead? He knows the raising up of Lazarus from the dead is far more glorious. "If thou believest, thou shalt see the glory of God."

(2) People Wishing to Teach the Lord

Case 1
"This ointment might have been sold . . .
and given to the poor"

Sometimes people not only voice their complaints against the Lord, they even think to instruct him. "To what purpose hath this waste of the ointment been made?" asked the disciples. "For this ointment might have been sold for above three hundred shillings, and given to the poor" (Mark 14.4,5). This was a case of teaching the Lord. The disciples could think of some other way to use the ointment—sell it and give the proceeds to the poor. The Lord, however, knew precisely what she was doing. So He said, "She hath wrought a good work on me." The Lord has never said a word or performed any act which He himself does not know. He needs no one to improve on Him. Only the foolish will ever dream of improving or instructing the Lord.

Case 2
"This shall never be unto thee"

During the time when the Lord showed the disciples how He must go to Jerusalem and be crucified, what did Peter say to Him? "Lord, this shall never be unto thee!" The Lord, though, answered, "Get thee behind me, Satan" (Matt. 16.21-23). Peter wished to instruct the Lord; whereas instead, his foolishness was being exposed.

Case 3
"What manner of woman this is"

Once the Lord Jesus was eating in the home of Simon, one of the Pharisees. A woman came and positioned herself behind the Lord at His feet—weeping, wetting His feet with her tears, and wiping them with the hair of her head. Simon spoke within himself, musing, "This man, if he were a prophet, would have perceived who and what manner of woman this is that toucheth him" (Luke 7.36-39). Let us contemplate Simon's spirit. He seemed to entertain the idea of telling the Lord: You should have at least judged what manner of woman this was before you allowed her to get near you and stand at your feet. Although Simon had not opened his mouth, the Lord knew his heart. Hence He told him the parable of forgiven much and forgiven little. What the Lord tried to convey to Simon was: You gave Me no water for my feet, because you felt little was forgiven; but she has wet My feet with tears because she felt much was forgiven. By obtaining such an impression as this, we can readily see how foolish it is for any man to try to be the Lord's counselor. We will also begin to know Jesus of Nazareth in a way we have never known Him before.

(3) The Lord Loving People to Ask
for Great Things

By carefully reading the Gospels we are impressed by how much the Lord loves people to ask of Him. The greater their demand the happier He is.

Sample 1
"If thou wilt, thou canst make me clean"

Let us look at the story of a leper found in Mark 1. According to Jewish law one who has leprosy is forbidden to have any contact with other people. Whoever touches a leper is himself defiled (see Lev. 13 and 14). Now a certain leper came to the Lord Jesus. Please note that this very coming was itself illegal. Oh do let us have the right impression here. Whenever a leper comes forth, we must immediately be sensitive about it. Unless one is willing to spend and be spent of himself, he will spontaneously react, saying: You come out to hurt me! Since I cannot have any contact with you, why do you come!?! This leper in coming did not ask the Lord for cleansing; he instead pleaded, "If thou wilt, thou canst make me clean." How strong was the plea. He placed all the responsibility on the Lord—it became purely a matter of whether or not He was willing. This was not an ordinary prayer; it tested the very heart of the Lord. Furthermore, the Lord could easily have just said a word to the leper and in that way make him clean, but He used His hand to touch the leper as well as He spoke the word, "I will; be thou made clean." What a risk! Suppose the leper were not made clean, then the Lord himself would be defiled! Yet how willing our Lord committed himself to the situation. He staked His own holiness and purity on His action taken toward the leper. Either they both were clean or they both were defiled; either both were cast out of the camp or both returned to the camp. Oh how gladly the Lord expended himself. What an expensive habit He had.

Sample 2
"Uncovered the roof"

Mark 2 narrates how four men brought a man sick of the palsy to the Lord Jesus. They could not get near for the crowd. So they "uncovered the roof" where the Lord was and let down the bed on which the sick of the palsy lay. Now let us again be rightly impressed with the situation: Here is the Lord, who must at this moment be extremely busy, for a needy crowd surrounded Him; nevertheless, these four men let down the palsied man through the roof. That day the Lord was using the house of others for preaching. How troublesome it must therefore be that these men would have to repair the roof once they had torn it apart. Far from warning them not to do this the next time, the Lord seemed to be pleased with their strong request. It seems as though the stronger the demand on Him the happier He is with it. Such is the way we come to know what a Lord He is. If we fail to ever catch such an impression how can we ever know Him?

Sample 3
"Jesus, thou son of David, have mercy on me"

As the Lord was walking out of Jericho, Bartimaeus cried out, "Jesus, thou son of David, have mercy on me" (Mark 10.47). Many rebuked him that he should hold his peace; but he cried out the more. So far as the Lord himself was concerned, He did not like such clamor. Is it not written, "He shall not strive, nor cry aloud; neither shall any one hear his voice in the streets" (Matt. 12.19)? Although He might have his own preference, even so, when a person clamors for Him to spend himself, He will gladly heal him. The Lord loves to have people open their mouths wide and ask big things of Him. How gladly He wills to dispense abounding grace.

Sample 4
"The dogs eat of the crumbs which
fall from their masters' table"

This principle of the Lord spending himself becomes even clearer in the case of the Canaanitish woman. The bread was prepared for the (Israelite) children; but, said this Gentile woman, "even the dogs eat of the crumbs which fall from their masters' table" (Matt. 15.27). Here was a demand beyond measure; yet the Lord was pleased with such a demand. He not only answered her prayer by healing her daughter but also praised her great faith. Many are such instances in the Gospels. If we correctly receive these impressions we shall be able to know the Lord's heart in these matters.

Sample 5
"I believe; help thou mine unbelief"

When the Lord Jesus came down from the mount of transfiguration, He met a father who brought his demon-possessed son with him. Now this man, it should be noted, was chided by the Lord (see Mark 9.14-29). The Lord had not reproved the leper who came to Him; nor had He rebuked the palsied man who came through the roof. On the contrary, He had been happy with their excessive demands. This father, it will be remembered, had brought his son first to the disciples, who had then failed to cast out the demon. So now he came to the Lord. When he was asked how long since this had happened to his son, the father answered, "From a child. And oft-times it hath cast him both into the fire and into the waters, to destroy him: but *if thou canst* do anything, have compassion on us, and help us." Taking up his word, the Lord Jesus said: "If thou canst! All things are possible to him that believeth." What the Lord meant was: you were asking "if thou canst"; you ought to know that "all things are possible to him that believeth." The problem lies in whether you believe, not in whether I can do.

Let us try to grasp the situation of that moment. This father was rather half-hearted. He had the heart to *come* to the Lord, but he did not *believe* in the Lord. He did not quite believe in His power, for he said, "If thou canst do anything." This word met with a severe reprimand from the Lord. Our Lord dislikes people making small requests of Him; He is not afraid of having people tell Him: Whether or not You are willing; or, You must do it. But the father's attitude here was: if You are able, fine; if You are not, leave it; Your disciples could not, so it will not really matter if You cannot either. In view of this attitude,

the Lord chided him, saying: You were still saying "if thou
canst"; but "all things are possible to him that believeth"!
In hearing this word, the father immediately cried out with
tears: "I believe; help thou mine unbelief"! Being repri-
manded and shown his fault, he turned to the Lord. Now
he believed, and by so doing he placed all responsibility
upon the Lord. How beautiful was the scene! The greater
the person's demand is, the happier is the Lord; the less
the demand, the greater becomes His displeasure. May we
be sensitive people who allow God to deposit these
impressions with us. And so shall we see that the Gospels
as a whole are full of the glory of the Lord.

c. *By Way of Uniqueness*

Instance 1
"Who is my neighbor?"

Let us take note of the principle point in the story of
the Samaritan. The question which a certain lawyer asked
was, "Who is my neighbor?" The answer the Lord Jesus
gave was totally opposite from the question asked. In verse
27 of Luke 10 it reads: "Thou shalt love . . . thy neighbor
as thyself." The neighbor must be another person; the
"you" or "thou" here should be the lawyer. What our
Lord meant was that you the lawyer ought to love your
neighbor as you love yourself the lawyer, and thus will you
inherit eternal life. Desiring to justify himself, the lawyer
next said to the Lord Jesus, "And who is my neighbor?"
He must have thought the Lord Jesus would tell him to
love other people. So he wished to find out who that
person was. However, after the Lord had finished telling
the story He finally raised the question: "Which of these
three, thinkest thou, proved neighbor unto him that fell

among the robbers?" The lawyer replied, "He that showed mercy on him." Jesus said, "Go, and do thou likewise." The lawyer asked "Who is my neighbor?"; the Lord answered with another question, "Which . . . proved neighbor unto him that fell among the robbers?" In other words, you the lawyer are the one who has fallen into the hands of robbers, and he who showed mercy to you is your neighbor. The neighbor here pointed to no other than the Savior. The Lord intended by this story to reveal to the lawyer that the neighbor was the Lord himself. "Go," said the Lord, "and do thou likewise." Love that Samaritan with all your heart.

Unfortunately many change the noble import of this story. They conclude that the Lord wants us to be that Samaritan, overlooking the fact that we cannot go to the cross to atone for sin nor can we be lifted up to cause the Holy Spirit to descend. Christ alone has the oil and wine. He alone has the beast. He alone has the inn, and He alone has the money. We are not the Samaritan. This passage means: I the Lord am your neighbor; I save you, I pour wine on you to forgive you, I pour oil on you to give you life, I set you on My own beast, I bring you to an inn which is the church, I give you the shilling that you may receive both gift and grace, till I come back to receive you. In commanding us to love the Samaritan, He is in reality asking us to love Him. Let us truly learn to touch the fine point of this passage; for only thus shall we be able to comprehend the story.

Instance 2
The Serene Glory of the Lord

When people came to the garden of Gethsemane to take Him, the Lord stepped forward and said to them,

"Whom seek ye?" "Jesus of Nazareth," they said. To which the Lord answered, "I am he." When He said "I am he" they went backward and fell to the ground (John 18.4-6). By speaking simply a word, these men fell backward to the ground. What glory can be seen here!

Our Lord prayed in the garden of Gethsemane, yet He asked for nothing in the courts—neither before the high priest nor before the governor. *This* Man is far above all. He is Lord, yet He was judged. Who were judging Him? That impetuous and impertinent high priest before whom our Lord kept still. That impatient governor who asked silly questions to which He answered not a word. Jesus of Nazareth is God. Although He was being judged, He did not lose His dignity nor His serenity.

In Gethsemane He asked the disciples to watch with Him (Matt. 26.38), but He did not request their prayers. Paul solicited the prayers of the brethren in Rome, yet the Lord never asked people to pray for Him. He is the Son of God; He needs no intercession. He wants His disciples to pray that *they* may not fall into temptation (Matt. 26.41); it is a request that they pray for themselves. Here do we perceive the dignity and serenity of the Lord.

He lived poorly on earth, yet He never begged for a penny. He pleaded with God in the garden, but He entreated no one in the court. Who is like the Son of God!?! Glorious indeed is the throne, glory too is manifested in judgment and the cross. Let us worship Him, saying: You are Lord, You are indeed Lord!

Instance 3
The Lord Does Not Display Himself

The Lord shuns display and does not seek fame. After He had healed the leper, He charged him not to tell anyone (Matt. 8.4). When He cast out a legion of demons He ordered the delivered person to return to his house and to declare how great things *God* had done for him (Luke 8.39). Having opened the eyes of the two blind men He strictly bade them not to let anybody know (Matt. 9.30). At the moment that God revealed Him as Christ to Peter He enjoined the disciples not to inform others that He was the Christ (Matt. 16.20). On the mount of transfiguration He for once manifested His glory; yet in coming down He commanded His disciples to tell the vision to no man (Matt. 17.9). In John 7 we have a similar instance. Not knowing Him, Jesus' own brothers in the flesh said to Him, "Depart hence, and go into Judea . . . For no man doeth anything in secret, and himself seeketh to be known openly. If thou doest these things, manifest thyself to the world." Even his brothers spoke such words because they did not believe in Him. "My time is not yet come" was His answer to them. Nevertheless, when his brethren had gone up, then He also went up to the feast, yet not publicly, but as it were in secret (vv. 2-10). He did not go up to perform miracles; rather, He went up to preach. Here again we touch His glory. For all who desire to attract human attention are anxious to set their works before men. Our Lord, though, never seeks to appear before men for self-display. The Gospels are full of such instances. Each time He stood before people, it was only to fulfill an absolute need. He was most reluctant to tell people who He was. Even after He had performed the miracle of giving sight to the blind He did not inform him immediately who He was until after the latter had been brought to a certain degree of understanding (see John 9). So let us really come to know the Lord.

3. *Impression through learning.*

In order to understand the histories in both the Old and the New Testament we need to receive impressions, which in turn require us to have delicate feelings. For this reason we must learn before God. For example, suppose there is a mean person here. How can he ever know the honor of the Lord Jesus when he reads the Gospels? Yet if he should receive some dealing from the Lord, and begin to understand a little what honor is, he will come to know something of the honor of the Lord Jesus as he reads the Bible. For that person who is totally ignorant of honor and glory, where or how can he ever get an impression of the Lord's honor and glory? It is for this reason that we need to learn before God. As the divine nature of God increases in us our feelings towards His word become more refined and our impressions grow deeper, and thus shall we better understand the word of God. May we remember one basic principle: "Whosoever hath, to him shall be given, and he shall have abundance: but whosoever hath not, from him shall be taken away even that which he hath" (Matt. 13.12). Our learning must not be slothful lest even what we have be taken away from us.

C. ENTERING INTO THE SPIRIT OF THE BIBLE.

In order to study the Bible well there is the further need of entering into the spirit of the Bible. This is additional to our entering into the thought and into the fact of the Holy Spirit.

1. *Touching the spirit behind the word.*

When the Spirit of God uses men to write the Bible—and whether touching facts or doctrines—there is in each of its books, nay, in each and every passage, the spirit of the Bible. For the Holy Spirit manifests His own feeling through the human spirit. When, for example, we say the joy of the Holy Spirit it is not the Holy Spirit himself who is joyful; rather, He is joyful in man's spirit. Or further, in mentioning the grief of the Holy Spirit it again is not the Holy Spirit himself who is grieved, but He is grieved in the spirit of man. In other words, as man's spirit joins in with the Holy Spirit the feeling of the Holy Spirit becomes that of man's spirit. And conversely, man's condition has become the condition of the Holy Spirit.

When God's Spirit engages men to write Biblical history it is more than a recording of factual occurrences. We must see that Biblical history is not only true but also spiritual: there is the feeling of the Holy Spirit in that particular narrative. Similarly, in the writing of the Epistles not only are doctrine and thought there but the feelings of the Holy Spirit behind them are there as well. Consequently, the Scriptures comprise more than facts and doctrines. At the fore is the word, and behind the word is the thought, but behind the thought is the spirit. If we only get to the word, such study of the Bible is extremely superficial. Yet if we are able to receive an impression—that is, if we get into its thought—the study becomes deeper. But should we stop at this step our understanding of the Scriptures is still quite limited. For behind each and every word of God there is both the spirit which tells of the feeling of the Holy Spirit as well as the condition of the writer at that particular moment. And those who study the Bible need to touch that very spirit.

The word and the spirit are inseparable. The ministry of the word is a releasing of the spirit. Whoever rises up to be a minister of the word must release his spirit; otherwise he cannot be one. The spirit must be right, and then he will have the ministry of the word. Oftentimes we fail in ministering the word because the spirit lags behind the word released. The word is correct, but the spirit is wrong. The word may be strong, yet the spirit is weak. Those in the Bible who are ministers of the word, though, do not have such a problem. Their spirit matches the substance they write. Behind every passage and behind each book they write is the appropriate spirit. To fulfill the ministry of the word requires the word at the fore and the spirit at the back. Moreover, for all to receive the ministry of the word, it requires them to touch the spirit behind the word given. As we read the Bible we are receiving the ministry of the word.

How necessary it is, then, for us to touch the spirit within the word; else our understanding of the Bible is bound to be very superficial, since all that we get may only be doctrines and facts which do not give us proper spiritual nourishment. If God's word is just impressions and thought, it cannot be our food; it has to be spirit in order for it to become food to us. Our food is obtained through touching the spirit in the word. The substance of the Bible is the spirit. Failure to touch the spirit behind a certain Scripture passage means failure in understanding that passage. Hence in studying the Scriptures we must touch the spirit—that very special spirit.

2. *How to touch the spirit behind the word.*

How do we touch the spirit behind the word? Let me say that it does not depend on human effort but on the discipline of the Holy Spirit. By His discipline the Spirit of God comes to substitute for man's work. What is the discipline of the Holy Spirit? It is God's Spirit arranging all our environments by which He works until our spirit becomes one with the spirit of the Bible. Although the two may not become *completely* the same, nevertheless they become at least *partially* alike in character. And thus shall we begin to touch the spirit of the Scriptures. Only a kindred spirit may touch the spirit of the Bible; an alien spirit cannot do so. Hence at the height of the study of the Bible, the spirit of the person who studies God's word is brought into one with the spirit of the person who has written it. And as their spirits merge, the spiritual substance of the Bible is unveiled.

The spirit behind the word of the Scriptures is quite unique. It is very definite. The Holy Spirit will use a person to write a portion of the Bible only after He has so worked in the person's life that He considers it usable. With such a perfect spirit the Holy Spirit is then able to release through him such words as are in fact found in the Bible. This means that when the Holy Spirit inspires the writing of the Scriptures He only gives words to that man whom He has prepared beforehand as a suitable vessel. Because this vessel has the proper spirit, therefore He causes him to write these words. So that at the back of the word of the Bible lies a human spirit that is perfect, strong and faultless, because the Holy Spirit has by now brought the spirit of that man to a point where it is not only satisfactory but also usable to Him. Not until the Holy Spirit is certain that His liberty will not be restricted by the man and that He is able to express His thought freely without any interference of any kind will He use this man in setting down the Scriptures. It is for this reason that we may declare that the word of the Bible is Holy Spirit-breathed. Although it comes from man's spirit, even so, when it comes forth it seems to be the Holy Spirit. This is because the Holy Spirit has perfect liberty in man. Man's spirit and the Holy Spirit are so joined together that there appears to be no more difference. Now since those who *write* the Bible must be brought by the Holy Spirit to such a degree, we who *read* the Bible also must be brought by the same Holy Spirit to the point where our spirit becomes one with the spirit of the writers who were then inspired. Only in this way will we touch the spirit behind God's word. Hence in studying the Bible we are not merely reading its words or simply understanding their meanings; we are engaged in an activity which requires that we be brought by the Lord to where our spirit can be merged with the spirit of the word.

The words of the Scriptures are letters and not sounds. Aside from the "Selah" in the Psalms, nowhere else in the whole Bible does it tell us when we should read softly or when we should read loudly. How then can we ever discern the feeling of the spirit if we do not know the softness or loudness of sound?

Many words in the Bible are found to be a pleading or a beseeching—just as would an evangelist who appeals from the pulpit imploring people to come to the Lord. He so pleads, perhaps, because he knows the woes of a sinner and the fateful destiny of such a person. Or perhaps he is so filled with the love of Christ that he longs for sinners to return to the Lord. It takes much love, sympathy and feeling to adequately put these pleadings into words. How can we understand what we read if we lack any one of these sentiments?

Some of the words in the Bible are those of reprimand. If a person has never been broken before God will he be able to comprehend these words of correction? He knows only sharp words spoken through ill-temper; he does not know admonition given out of a burdened spirit. He does not realize that although outwardly both are words of rebuke, the spirit behind each is vastly different one from the other.

We must learn to touch the spirit of the Bible with our

spirit. With a view to training our spirit, the Holy Spirit orders our environments. Let us recognize that the discipline of the Holy Spirit is the primary and very best training of our life. Such training is in His hand, not in ours. He disciplines us intermittently, with one exercise following another, until our spirit is brought to the proper state. Our spirit is being dealt with in a variety of ways and at different moments: here a blow and there some joy; here a little patience and there something forsaken; and thus are we led to a condition not unlike that condition we read about in a particular passage of the Bible. Our spirit has been trained to such a degree of suitability that even though the meaning of the word has not increased, the inward understanding seems to be clear and thorough. When we speak of it we know what we are talking about, for we have become quite clear as to what it is. We are not only clear in meaning or in word, we are clear in spirit. It is consequently deeper than word and meaning. Our spirit is being brought by the Spirit of God into a oneness with the spirit of His word.

So with regard to this matter of touching the spirit of the word of the Bible, it is not a question of method but a question of the man being dealt with. If our spirit has not been brought into oneness with the spirit of the writer of the Bible, we can at most be teachers but cannot at all be prophets. The most we touch will be teachings or doctrines but not the spirit. Unless we are dealt with by God and are disciplined, we will be reading the Bible as though behind a veil. No matter how we read, we will be far off. Our spirit must be strictly dealt with by God.

During the first few years of our studying God's word, we may indeed be able to comprehend a few doctrines and understand a few facts. But to touch the spirit is not as easy a matter because our spirit is not yet prepared and remains unusable. It takes considerable time—at least a few years—for our spirit to be adjusted properly, being stricken and broken so as to be conformed to the particular state or condition called for by any particular Scripture passage. As a matter of fact, it requires a considerable period of time for our spirit to be brought into oneness with the spirit of the Bible. To enter into its spirit man's wisdom is absolutely no help. Human wisdom may aid us in grasping the word quicker, but it cannot assist us in touching the spirit behind the word. No matter how strong is our imagination and our power of comprehension, these are unable to get us into the spirit of the word. It requires the Holy Spirit to bring us into harmony with the spirit of the word.

3. *From same quality to expanded capacity.*

The Holy Spirit works in us so that our spirit may approach sameness with the spirit of the Bible. This, however, points merely to the sameness of quality, not to the sameness in capacity. The Spirit of the Lord Jesus surpasses us to the nth degree. For He is the only begotten Son of God. To have the same quality simply means that as He has that kind of Spirit so we have something of this same kind of spirit too. Though of the same kind, nevertheless not to the same degree.

Even so, the discipline of the Holy Spirit enlarges our spirit's capacity besides conforming us to the spirit of the Bible. The Lord uses His Spirit to enlarge our spirit. This is called nourishing. Such "feeding" goes on incessantly. He gives us a little today, a little more after a few days. By adding gradually, our spirit is expanded. So that with the understanding of the Bible comes the nourishing, and in turn the enlarged capacity. *The starting point of knowing the Scriptures is in the sameness of the spirit's quality; while the concluding stage in knowing the Scriptures is the enlargement of the spirit's capacity.*

An example of this may be helpful here. A person may easily lose his temper. However much he reads God's word, he just cannot take it in. Later on, though, he is smitten of God, and thus he learns something of patience. This is not a deliberate trying to be patient—not a humanly manufactured patience; rather, it is the work of the Holy Spirit. It comes spontaneously. Now upon reading the word of God once again after having touched such a spirit, he will then receive the supply of Christ. God's word will support his spirit that he may receive more abundantly. Time after time a supply of Christ is being added to him.

We see then that the discipline of the Holy Spirit causes the spirit of man first to become the same in quality with the spirit of the Bible and next to have its capacity expanded. Such enlargement is partly due to the discipline in environment and partly due to the word of the Holy Spirit in the Bible. The Holy Spirit does the work of breaking down by the discipline in environment; but He also supplies us with the word of the Bible that we may be enlarged in our capacity. Whenever the Holy Spirit supplies us with His word, we gain a little more. By the continuous supply of His word, the Holy Spirit is able to expand our capacity endlessly.

As we are nourished by the Bible we feel that the word is forever fresh. From the human standpoint the Bible was written about nineteen hundred years ago. But besides showing us the thought and concept of that time, can there possibly be shown to us anything else of its characteristic? We need to recognize the fact that the Spirit of the Bible of that time is still with us today. As we currently read the Bible, it seems as if it has just been written. For each time we use our spirit to read it, we always feel refreshed. Though the Book is already possessed of a history of almost nineteen hundred years, it still has not become old. Many books turn tasteless after being read a few times, but the Bible is still new even after dozens of times of use. Why is this so? Because it is in the Spirit. If we read this book according to the letter we shall soon find it aged; the same will be true if we merely try to think on it. But if we read the Bible by our spirit, we will feel refreshed each time we read. Whenever a passage of Scripture appears meaningless to us we need to realize it is not the Bible that is being meaningless here; rather, it is our spirit being inadequate, since each passage of the Bible is full of spirit. Were our spirit sufficient we would sense the preciousness of every passage. Unless we read the Scriptures with the spirit we shall not obtain much, even should we select Romans or the Sermon on the Mount. So here is not a case of the Bible lacking meaning, but a case of our spirit having fallen. Once our spirit drops down, the Scriptures immediately become flat and turn tasteless. If the spirit is inadequate, it is impossible to savor the sweetness of the Bible. But with a strong spirit, the Book instantly becomes fresh as though having just been written.

Who knows how rich is the spirit in the Bible? Do not assume that your spirit is adequate, or that you are able to cope with demands from all sides. Only those who have been dealt with know a little of the Bible. According to the measure of the dealings we have will be the degree of our understanding. Because of the limit of our dealings, many places in the Scriptures remain unknown to us today just as they were several years ago. For this reason, we must have the discipline of the Holy Spirit. With one more discipline received, a little more learning is obtained inwardly. As we learn to a certain point whereby our spirit begins to be identified with the spirit of God's word, we shall see light, receive revelation, and be fed.

4. *Our spirit must be sensitive.*

Why is it that in reading the same passage of Scripture you find it most precious, whereas another brother feels differently? This is because you grasp the spirit of this passage but the other brother does not. Not that he has no spirit; only, his spirit is not in tune with the spirit of this particular passage. Yet please note that it is possible for him to sense the preciousness of *another* Scripture passage, while you see nothing in it. For this reason, the spirit in each one of us needs to be sensitive and delicate so as to produce various feelings for different situations. The more delicate and sensitive the spirit, the more comprehensive the understanding of the Bible. Whether one's understanding of the Bible is broad or narrow, great or small, depends on how much the discipline of the Holy Spirit has been received. Only as we receive much discipline does our sensitivity become rich and delicate. Only through increasing discipline is our sensitivity heightened. To have received a certain kind of discipline helps us to understand a certain passage in God's word. It is therefore immensely important to have abundant dealings. Without abundant dealings there will be no rich feelings. If spiritual feeling is not rich, the understanding of the Bible cannot be abounding.

5. *Two examples.*

Let us now illustrate what is meant by entering into the spirit of the Bible by taking two examples from the Word.

Example 1
The Story of Jacob

Jacob was naturally clever, crafty, and selfish. In every thing he thought first of himself instead of other people. He was full of schemes. It could be said of him that he would use all kinds of ways to achieve his aim. Because of this, God dealt with him. When he was born, he held on to his brother's heel and strove with his brother. But Esau was favored by his father whereas he was not. He used every means to steal his brother's blessing; yet what he got was wandering instead of blessing. He served Laban, but Laban changed his wages ten times. He wished to marry Rachel but was forced to marry Leah first. Later on, while he was traveling towards his father's house, Rachel died whereas Leah lived on. He favored some of his sons, especially Joseph; unexpectedly Joseph was sold by his own brethren. The latter dipped Joseph's coat of many colors into blood to deceive Jacob into thinking that his son Joseph had been devoured by an evil beast. He mourned for his son, saying: "I will go down to Sheol to my son mourning" (Gen. 37.35). Thereafter he pinned all his hopes on his youngest son Benjamin; and, behold, Benjamin was brought down to Egypt! Thus Jacob was dealt with by God daily; he lived a rather rugged life. Truly, "the way of the transgressor is hard" (Prov. 13.15). His ungodly and crafty days were full of evil indeed.

Let us not consider the experience of Jacob at Peniel as something casual or insignificant. For at that moment he insisted that God bless him. He seemed to be saying that since his father must bless him, and everybody else must bless him, so God must bless him too. He was such a crafty person that he must reap something each time. God gave him a promise, saying: "Thy name shall be called

Israel." But it took some time before he actually became Israel. Now at Peniel, as God touched his thigh, he was crippled. The work of God upon him began to take a turn. Yet on the second day afterwards, when he was to meet Esau, it was the same old Jacob. He divided his children into groups, with his beloved Joseph and Rachel at the last—so that in case the first group was attacked, the others might survive. He still leaned on his cleverness; he still possessed his scheming ways.

Nonetheless, however crafty he once had been, when he was advanced in age he became a man with tremendous spirituality. How very different he now was as he journeyed to Egypt. Exactly how? "Joseph brought in Jacob his father, and set him before Pharaoh: and Jacob blessed Pharaoh" (Gen. 47.7). How exquisite was this scene. Pharaoh was the master of the nation; but as he stood before Jacob, Pharaoh descended while the latter man ascended. When the one who had obtained rest after several decades of struggles stood up, even Pharaoh the master of a nation had to yield. Had it been as in former days, Jacob would probably have lusted after Pharaoh's things as soon as he met Pharaoh. Had he not earlier done that to Laban? Although Pharaoh's possessions surpassed Laban's a thousand times over, Jacob could nonetheless stand before him as one who had been smitten, who now naturally thought of the lesson learned before God rather than of the things which Pharaoh had.

"And Pharaoh said unto Jacob, How many are the days of the years of thy life? And Jacob said unto Pharaoh, The days of the years of my pilgrimage are a hundred and thirty years; few and evil have been the days of the years of my life, and they have not attained unto the days of the years of the life of my fathers in the days of their pilgrimage" (Gen. 47.8-9). Here the spirit of this man had come forth. He confessed, "Few and evil have been the days of the years of my life." This statement told the whole story of his life. Only after much smiting was this person, now aged, able to utter these words. If our spirit joins in with his spirit, we will see that one who has been smitten is never haughty. Let us recall how God had promised Abraham, saying, "I will make thy seed as the dust of the earth" (Gen. 13.16); how He had also promised Isaac: "I will multiply thy seed as the stars of heaven" (Gen. 26.4). During those days there was neither a house nor a race, only an individual. With Jacob today, though, his household numbered seventy people. God's promise had now been fulfilled so far as the "house" was concerned. Yet Jacob thought nothing of it; instead he confessed, "They have not attained unto the days of the years of the life of my fathers in the days of their pilgrimage." Having been smitten, he truly became humble.

"And Jacob blessed Pharaoh, and went out from the presence of Pharaoh" (Gen. 47.10). When Jacob came in, he blessed Pharaoh; now in going out he blessed Pharaoh again. How beautiful it was that he had something to give to others. The aged Jacob was totally different from his former self. This day he had truly become Israel. Here do we need to touch his spirit. "And Jacob lived in the land of Egypt seventeen years: so the days of Jacob, the years of his life, were a hundred forty and seven years. And the time drew near that Israel must die." We should note that when he was born he had been named Jacob, but when he died he was called Israel.

"And he called his son Joseph, and said unto him, If now I have found favor in thy sight, put, I pray thee, thy hand under my thigh, and deal kindly and truly with me: bury me not, I pray thee, in Egypt; but when I sleep with

my fathers, thou shalt carry me out of Egypt, and bury me
in their burying-place. And he said, I will do as thou hast
said. And he said, Swear unto me: and he sware unto him.
And Israel bowed himself upon the bed's head" (Gen.
47.28-31). How lovely is this picture! May we touch the
spirit here. Here was one who naturally was sly and
difficult, always striving to gain the utmost advantage;
today, though, he says to his son, "If now I have found
favor in thy sight." How soft he has become: "Deal kindly
and truly with me"—he asks for love and for truth. "Bury
me not, I pray thee, in Egypt"; for the land that God had
promised to him was Canaan, and God's promise was not
to be fulfilled in Egypt. All this shows how clear Jacob was
at his dying moment. What he meant was: I am of God's
people and am under God's discipline. I am now dying, so
please deal kindly and truly with me—bury me in the
promised land of God. He was not disbelieving God's
promise at all; but because of his believing, he asked
Joseph to swear that his son might recognize the solemnity
of the matter. We will not be able to understand if we do
not touch his spirit. How very precious was the fact that
"Israel bowed himself upon the bed's head".

The story of Jacob continues on in Genesis 48. "And
one told Jacob, and said, Behold thy son Joseph cometh
unto thee: and Israel strengthened himself, and sat upon
the bed. And Jacob said unto Joseph, God Almighty
appeared unto me at Luz in the land of Canaan, and
blessed me, and said unto me, Behold, I will make thee
fruitful, and multiply thee, and I will make of thee a
company of peoples, and will give this land to thy seed
after thee for an everlasting possession" (vv.2-4). He
remembered all God had promised him. He clearly
understood that his having seventy people in his household was God's blessing, for had not God promised him

that he should be fruitful and that his seed would possess the land of Canaan?

"And now thy two sons, who were born unto thee in the land of Egypt before I came unto thee into Egypt, are mine; Ephraim and Manasseh, even as Reuben and Simeon, shall be mine" (v.5). Jacob took the two sons of Joseph as his own sons and put them in God's promise. At his advanced age, he was obscure in nothing.

"And as for me, when I came from Paddan, Rachel died by me" (v.7). This incident had previously touched him most deeply. Even in his dying hour, he still remembered this episode. How gentle, matured and sweet now was he who had been scourged! How rich were his resources! That oily Jacob had become another person.

"And Israel beheld Joseph's sons, and said, Who are these? And Joseph said unto his father, They are my sons, whom God hath given me here. And he said, Bring them, I pray thee, unto me, and I will bless them. Now the eyes of Israel were dim for age, so that he could not see" (vv.8-10a). We will recall that when Isaac became old and his eyes grew dim, he had been deceived. Now Jacob too was old and eyes were dim, yet his inward eyes were most bright. Not as Isaac who in old age was gluttonous for venison; instead, Jacob was desirous to bless. "And [Joseph] brought them near unto him; and he kissed them, and embraced them" (v.10b). How full was the tender mercy of this elderly person.

"And Israel said unto Joseph, I had not thought to see thy face: and, lo, God hath let me see thy seed also" (v.11). Here we are shown again the broken spirit of one who had been stricken.

"And Joseph brought them out from between his knees; and he bowed himself with his face to the earth. And Joseph took them both, Ephraim in his right hand toward Israél's left hand, and Manasseh in his left hand toward Israel's right hand, and brought them near unto him. And Israel stretched out his right hand, and laid it upon Ephraim's head, who was the younger, and his left hand upon Manasseh's head, guiding his hands wittingly; for Manasseh was the first-born" (vv.12-14). "And when Joseph saw that his father laid his right hand upon the head of Ephraim, it displeased him . . . And Joseph said unto his father, Not so, my father; for this is the first-born; put thy right hand upon his head. And his father refused, and said, I know it, my son, I know it; he also shall become a people, and he also shall be great: howbeit his younger brother shall be greater than he, and his seed shall become a multitude of nations" (vv.17-19). Though his eyes were dim, his inside was not a bit muddled. He knew what God wanted him to do. "And he blessed them that day, saying, In thee will Israel bless, saying, God make thee as Ephraim and as Manasseh: and he set Ephraim before Manasseh" (v.20). Let us be certain to note that while the blessing of Isaac was obscure, the blessing of Jacob was most transparent.

"And Israel said unto Joseph, Behold, I die: but God will be with you, and bring you again unto the land of your fathers" (v.21). This is faith. How real is living faith. Judging by the current circumstances, it would appear that all their future lay in Egypt, for there had not been any one family who had fared better than they. Despite this, Jacob declares: "God will be with you, and bring you again unto the land of your fathers. Moreover I have given unto thee one portion above thy brethren, which I took out of the hand of the Amorite with my sword and with my bow" (v.22). What he meant was: even though you, Joseph, are today the prime minister of Egypt, your land will not be in Egypt but in Canaan.

Furthermore, Genesis 49 constitutes one of the greater prophecies in the Bible. There Jacob prophesied the future of each of the twelve tribes. He blessed them according to faith and obedience. Everything was crystal clear.

"And he charged them, and said unto them, I am to be gathered unto my people: bury me with my fathers in the cave that is in the field of Ephron the Hittite, in the cave that is in the field of Machpelah, which is before Mamre" (vv.29,30). "And when Jacob made an end of charging his sons, he gathered up his feet into the bed, and yielded up the ghost, and was gathered unto his people" (v.33). As he was being born, Jacob had been rather busy, seizing the heel of his brother; but as he was dying, he gathered up his feet into the bed. Leisurely and restful was he now, for he today had no controversy with God.

We need to realize that the Bible is full of spirit. If we use our spirit to touch that spirit we will find the word to be most sensitive and precious. We must contact with our spirit the spirit which is behind the letter of the Bible. Not the story nor the teaching alone, but the spirit of it as well.

Example 2
Paul in 2 Corinthians

Of the epistles of Paul, the one in which his spirit is released the most is probably 2 Corinthians. In his other epistles he mainly declares to us how much revelation he has received from God; but in this epistle God reveals the man Paul to us. His other epistles deal largely with his ministry, but this one speaks of his manner of life. It allows us to touch his spirit—how rich, how clean, and how gentle. Nowhere is Paul being misunderstood so much as in Corinth. All kinds of things are being spoken by the

Corinthians against him, nonetheless the spirit in which he answers them is transparent and pure beyond measure. It may be said that Paul's spirit is released more abundantly at the time he is misunderstood by the Corinthians than at the time he is being judged as recorded in the last few chapters of the book of Acts. If we slowly read the whole second epistle to the Corinthians sentence by sentence, we will be able to know his spirit as well as his thought. We will see that even when Paul is reproving, his spirit is not in anger. Indeed, only those who are full of love are qualified to reprove. If our spirit fails to be joined with Paul's spirit in 2 Corinthians, we shall misconstrue him as being boastful towards the Corinthians—as turning sour within himself. How we need to discern the possibility of there being two totally different spirits behind the same word. Man's word and meaning may be the same, yet the spirit can be quite different.

The above are just two of many examples. As a matter of fact the entire Bible is full of spirit, though some places may be more apparent in this regard than others. Whenever we read the Bible our spirit must be joined to its spirit. How can we understand those passages which narrate the many temptations Moses suffered if we are unable to enter into his spirit during those trials? How can we read the book of Psalms, which is more profound than the book of Jeremiah, if our spirit fails to join in with the spirit of the Psalms? Just so, we will not be able to study the New Testament either if our spirit falls behind the spirit of the New Testament.

For this reason, we need to learn some basic lessons before God. We need to be spiritual in order to read the Bible. We must have consecration that we may study the

Bible. We should not be subjective, nor careless, nor curious; rather must we learn to receive impressions from the facts and enter into the thought of the Holy Spirit.

Moreover, having all these we yet need to have our being so dealt with that our spirit is able to catch up with the spirit in each passage of the Bible. It requires a right kind of spirit to understand the word of God. In case we fail to touch the spirit, all that we see shall be mere letter. We may even misunderstand God's word and turn it topsy-turvy. Such a situation may be likened to a father who converses with several of his children: Should one of the children fail to touch the father's spirit, that child may pass on words which are according to his own fancy and not the truth, and so tell a totally different story from what is called for. Since the word of the Bible is full of spirit, we will not be able to know its feeling nor intent if we neglect the spirit. And as a result we may even misconstrue the content. Let us reiterate that should the person not be dealt with, there is no possibility of his studying the Bible well. Always remember that the proper avenue to our studying the Scriptures lies in our having dealings before God.

PART TWO

THE METHODS OF BIBLE STUDY

The Methods of Bible Study

Stress was laid in the previous part on the person who studies the Bible; we shall now emphasize the methods of studying the Bible. In studying God's word it requires proper method as well as the right person. In this second part that follows we shall be considering various methods of Bible study. And we shall view them from three different angles; namely, the keys to Bible study, the practices in Bible study, and the plans for Bible study.

1 | Keys to Bible Study

A. SEARCHING.

"Ye search the scriptures" (John 5.39). "Now the Beroeans were more noble than those in Thessalonica . . . examining the scriptures daily" (Acts 17.11).

The first thing to do in studying the Bible is to search the word of God. In other words, if we wish to get anything from the Bible we must go there and search for it, just as would anyone having lost something ransack through the bottom of the trunk to find it. We examine many things in order to search out the one thing we are looking for. Among God's many words there is one word which we today need, one word which will give us spiritual help at a particular moment, one word which will interpret or express the revelation we receive, or one word which will tell us what God's past revelation on a certain matter is.

Now in order to find this one word we have to search God's word. We need to adopt an attitude of searching when we read the Bible. To search simply indicates to read carefully, slowly, and unhurriedly. No word is skipped over without attempting to understand. Questions such as the following should be asked while reading: When was this word written? Who wrote it? To whom was it written? Under what circumstance was it written? What kind of feeling does it contain? Why was such a word written? What was the purpose of this word when written? As we deliberately ask these questions we search out carefully for the answers until we find them.

Sometimes in answering one question we will have to search meticulously through every word in the Old and New Testaments having any bearing on it. We must inspect very carefully lest we miss out on something important. There are times when we know what we are looking for in the word of God, but there are other times when we do not even know what we are looking for. Sometimes we look for one thing, sometimes we look for many things. Hence this matter of searching needs to be most careful and scrupulous, not letting even one word thoughtlessly slip away. Remember that the Scriptures are inspired of God. By inspiration is meant that every word in the Scriptures is God's word and therefore full of life. Hence we must study it most carefully.

Patience is needed in the study of the Bible. If there is any point we do not understand we can wait until we read it the second time. However, we must study it until we know it. Should we receive enlightenment from God at the first time let us be thankful. But if we are not given light at the first, we must carefully search for it—even to the hundredth time. Whenever we encounter some passage we do not understand, let us not become anxious. Do not try to comprehend it by forcing our mental power, nor feel compulsive to ask for light. For whatever comes out of the brain is not "amened" by the spirit. Indeed, the teaching conjured up by the mind is abominable to the spirit. For this reason do not read God's word merely with the mind. Be patient and search persistently until that day when God's time will have come for it to be shown to us.

A grave defect experienced by many people is that instead of searching the Scriptures themselves they read what others have had to say. No matter how much help others may render us, it is important that we study and search ourselves. We should not expect to receive help from others in lieu of ourselves studying the Bible. On the one hand we do not despise prophesying, since we do need the helps of prophecy and other ministries; but on the other hand we must read the Bible ourselves and not depend exclusively on other people's words.

B. RECITATION.

"Let the word of Christ dwell in you richly" (Col. 3.16). In order to store the word of Christ richly in the heart, the least one must do is to recite God's word. It goes without saying that rehearsing the Scriptures does not necessarily store up the word of God in the heart, but not rehearsing it will certainly not store the word of God in the heart either. Should a person merely recount the Bible with his mind while neither his heart is open to receive nor is he an obedient and tender man, then though he has indeed recounted the Bible he has not deposited God's word in his heart. Yet contrariwise, the man who is gentle, obedient, open and receptive but fails to memorize God's word is likewise not able to store it in the heart.

"Remember the words of the Lord Jesus, that he himself said, It is more blessed to give than to receive," said Paul to the Ephesian believers (Acts 20.35). In order to remember the Lord's word one needs to recite it, else how can he recall it? While He was on earth the Lord

Jesus too had memorized Scripture. He was able to quote freely the words in Deuteronomy to combat Satan's temptations. As He entered the synagogue in Nazareth He could immediately open the book of Isaiah to the place where was written His commission from God. These instances indicate that our Lord himself was well versed in the Bible. How much more we should carefully read the Bible and diligently memorize it. What purpose will it serve if we forget whatever we read?

The young people in particular ought to read the Bible with a searching attitude, but at the same time engage in memory work. During the first few years after being saved great effort should be made to memorize Scripture. Lots of passages need to be recited, such as Psalm 23, Psalm 91, Matthew 5, 6 and 7, John 15, Luke 15, 1 Corinthians 13, Romans 2 and 3, Revelation 2 and 3, and so forth. Those with good memory can perhaps memorize ten or so odd verses a day, while people with a weak memory can at least remember one verse. If a person spends five to ten minutes each day in reading a verse, searching and memorizing it, he will be able to finish such books like Galatians or Ephesians in approximately six months, Philippians in about four months, Hebrews in around ten months, and the Gospels such as John in nearly eighteen months. Should young brothers and sisters commence to read the Bible carefully at the start and recite at least one verse each day, they can without doubt memorize nearly all the main parts of the New Testament within four years. Such progress as outlined here has reference to people with weak memory. Those with a strong memory do not need so much time as this for achieving such a goal. In any case, such exercise can provide a very good foundation for the understanding of the New Testament.

Were our heart open to God and our attitude gentle we

would find no trouble in reciting Scripture. Were we to ponder on the Lord's word often, we could easily memorize the Bible. Whenever we are not occupied, let us recite the Scriptures and thus store the word of Christ richly in our heart. But should we not store the word of the Bible in our heart, the Holy Spirit will be faced with great difficulty in speaking to us. For each time God gives us revelation He usually makes use of the word in the Bible. If we do not remember the word of the Bible we tend to limit the coming of revelation. Consequently, in our mind should dwell the word of God. Reciting the Bible is not merely for the sake of recitation but is as preparation for receiving revelation. The more familiar we are with the Bible and the more passages we remember, the easier for the Holy Spirit to speak to our spirit. In reciting, do not rehearse the thought but the word. Our recitation needs to be exact and clear.

Besides those Scripture passages mentioned before, there are other important places in the Word which need to be carefully read together. For example: the journey of the children of Israel is very important, but so too is the route whereby Elisha followed Elijah. The missionary trips of Paul and the itinerary of Peter should be carefully noted and remembered. If we can recollect the various places where the Lord Jesus labored both in Judea and in Galilee, we will have a clear idea of the work of our Lord found in the Gospels. For His work was done partly in Judea and partly in Galilee. Also, the seven feasts and the six offerings in Leviticus should be memorized. In addition, if we can recall the two prayers of Paul in Ephesians and the ten times he made mention of the Holy Spirit we will be very greatly helped. All these are basic items. In memorizing these passages we shall see a little more of the riches of God's word. And of course there are many many

other passages like these which we can memorize. To sum
up, then, recite chapter by chapter all the important
Scriptures, recite verse by verse all the fragments, and
above all, recite the order of the sixty-six books of the
Bible.

C. COMPARISON.

Beyond searching and recitation, there is also the need
to compare Scriptures.

In 1 Corinthians 2 Paul speaks of spiritual things and
spiritual men. We shall see some new light if we compare
these two items.

Psalm 36.9 says, "In thy light shall we see light." Just
having light is not sufficient; our problem cannot be
solved until we have two lights, the one light leading to the
other light. Lights are complementary to each other.

2 Peter 1.20 states that "no prophecy of scripture is of
private interpretation." We may easily mistake it to mean
that no prophecy is to be interpreted according to private
or personal opinion. Yet the grammar of Peter's word
refers not to the person but to "its own particular
interpretation" (see Darby's translation). Should the passage mean no private interpretation of prophecy by the
reader, Peter would be speaking rather naïvely here, since
every Christian recognizes that already and needs not to
be reminded by him. But as a matter of fact, what Peter
means here by private interpretation is an interpreting
within a prophecy's own particular passage or place of
Scripture. No prophecy of Scripture should be interpreted
locally according to its own particular thought. In other
words, God never finishes all He wishes to say in just one
place or passage. Has not the prophet told us that the
word of God is "here a little, there a little" (Is. 28.13)?

Therefore no one who reads the Bible should interpret a passage by its own local meaning. To do so would be to engage in private interpretation. For instance, we must not explain either Daniel 9 or Revelation 13 by itself; for to explain it that way would be to violate the law of interpretation of prophecy. We instead should explain them together.

God shows us here a principle: that in reading a passage in the Scriptures we must compare it with other passages and not interpret just the one passage according to its own local meaning. Having possibly seen the teaching in one passage, we need to search for its interpretation in other passages. This is of great importance, since most of the heresies in Christianity have resulted from a seizing upon one or two Scripture verses without searching out all the other related Bible passages. Do recall that Satan quoted isolated Scripture verses too, and utilized them to tempt people. Let us remember that the more we compare, the less will there be private interpretation. If we are able to find ten additional verses to compare with the one verse we are reading, this will be much more dependable than finding only five for comparative purposes. The more comparison the better. Extra care should be taken if we have but just one verse. Do not inadvertently construct something big upon it, lest there be danger of falling into error.

As another example, in Revelation 19, where the Lord is recorded as one day coming down from heaven to make war, the reader learns that out of His mouth there proceeds a sharp sword with which He shall smite the nations. If this passage is interpreted on the basis of only this one verse, we would most likely end up saying that there is an actual sword in the mouth of our Lord, with that sword being a sharp one. But if we know that no prophecy of Scripture is to be privately interpreted, then we will try to discover from other verses what the sharp sword out of His mouth really refers to. And there in Ephesians 6.17 we learn that it points to the word of God.

Again, who are the ten virgins in Matthew 25? By considering 2 Corinthians 11.2 we come to see that the virgins refer to the church. (In 2 Corinthians the word "virgin" is singular, since it points to the one church; in Matthew, though, the virgins are ten in number, for they lay stress on the individual responsibility of each before God. "Ten" is the sum of two "fives"; and "five" is the Biblical number denoting man's responsibility before God). Such comparative study will give us much light.

It is also essential to compare together the New and the Old Testaments. If we are able to find out how far God speaks in the Old Testament and where the word of God ends in the New Testament, we shall perceive that God's word is progressive and His revelation is continuous. Many words are found in both the Old and the New Testaments. Take the book of Revelation for example. Without the book of Daniel there can be no book of Revelation; but in comparing these two books together, we realize that the latter book is more advanced than the former. Or take Revelation 2 and 3 and compare them with Matthew 13. Or take Revelation 4 and 5 and compare them with Philippians 2. Or take Revelation 6 and compare it first with Matthew 24, and then with Daniel. Through comparison and mutual interpretation, we are given to see what we have never seen before.

Similarly, the four Gospels may be chosen to illustrate this point. Great significance is lodged in the fact that some events are recorded in all the four Gospels while some others are not. For instance, Matthew does not narrate the ascension of the Lord Jesus but ends his narration with resurrection. Mark, however, speaks of the ascension of the Lord Jesus. Luke not only mentions the Lord's ascension but also predicts the descension of the Holy Spirit. John makes no reference at all to the ascension of the Lord Jesus, yet he does allude to the coming again of the Lord. Thus the ending of each narrative is different. We would like to ask why. And if we search for the answer, we shall find it. Matthew does not write about ascension because he stresses the uninterrupted rule of Christ on earth as King. Mark does record the ascension because it is proper for the Servant sent by God to return to God. Luke speaks on the glorified Man, and so he describes not only ascension but also the outpouring of the Holy Spirit. But John cannot report the ascension since he shows Christ as being still in heaven, the only begotten Son in the bosom of the Father forever. By thus comparing them, we will discover the characteristics of each Gospel.

D. MEDITATION.

Both Joshua 1.8 and Psalm 1.2 instruct us that man ought always to meditate on the word of the Lord. Even at the time when we are not reading the Bible we should still meditate on the Lord's word so as to have our thought transformed into the thought of the Bible. Whether at times of reading or at hours of not reading, we must with equal endeavor ponder God's word. "The mind of the Spirit" in Romans 8.6 means not just thinking of the Spirit, but even being spiritually minded. In other words, the mind will invariably turn to the word of God. Regardless the circumstance, our mind is set on God's word. Not because we force our mind to think about God's word, but rather we cannot help but be set on God.

For our daily thought is tuned to the thought of the Bible. Whether we are thinking or not thinking, our mind is occupied with the Bible. We spontaneously find ourselves inclining to God's word.

Therefore meditation has two aspects: one is our thought while reading the Bible, the other is our thought in our daily life. We ponder God's word during our reading, and we exercise our disciplined mind while not reading. Hence there is no need to exert ourselves in order to think on God's word, for the Holy Spirit will guide us into such thought. It has almost become our habit. And naturally, we will be enriched before God.

2 | Practices in Bible Study

A. TIME ARRANGEMENT.

Each one who studies the Bible must set aside a certain time for studying (this is in addition to the morning watch). Now experience teaches us that more time does not necessarily mean better result. Setting apart too much time does not often continue for very long, thus producing an adverse effect. Let us therefore decide on a standard which is generally workable. For those who serve the Lord, their daily study of the Bible *need not exceed two hours but should not be less than one hour.* Sometimes this may be extended to three hours if they have leisure time. Such an arrangement should be personally considered before any decision is made. But once decided upon, it should be practiced for a few years. Do not change it in less than two or three months. We must learn to discipline ourselves. There needs to be a definite arrangement, not random reading. Never imitate the "genius" type of casual reading. Many are too careless in studying the Bible. Today they may read for hours, tomorrow not for even one hour! With absolutely no sign of perseverance, it is a bad habit. Hence we should consider carefully and decide after much prayer concerning the time arrangement, and once the standard is set we should diligently keep it.

Suppose the decision is made to set aside one hour each day. How should this hour be used? This requires some further arrangement. It is best to divide the time into several sections, using different methods of studying. Some study methods are like the planting of trees that require eight to ten years before the result is seen. Other study methods are like the planting of vegetables or squashes which can be harvested annually. People may become discouraged by long-term reading, so that such reading should be mixed with the short-term kind that produces results in two to three months. And this will give beginners some comfort. To devote a whole hour to one thing can easily exhaust a person, hence it is better to divide up the hour into several sections.

First Section—The Study of Some Weightier Matters.

Suppose the first section is twenty minutes long. This twenty minutes should be used to study some weightier matters in the Bible. It will take several years before any result is seen. Study done on such subjects as types or the death of the Lord Jesus may take years to garner any harvest. Other subjects such as the so-called Sermon on the Mount in the Gospel according to Matthew, the prophecies and the parables in Matthew 13, the departing words of our Lord in the Gospel of John, the dispensational teaching, and so forth require months and years to obtain any fruit. To lay a good foundation for an understanding of the Old Testament, study at least such books as Genesis, Daniel, Exodus, Leviticus, Joshua, and in addition a prophetic book like Zechariah. For the New

Testament, Matthew is the first book to study, followed by Romans, Revelation, and Hebrews, and to then be continued by a study of John, Ephesians, and Galatians. Such study will not produce an instant result. But after reading them through dozens of times, there may be some gleanings. So then, undertake this kind of reading during the first time section. Since during this first segment our mind is usually keenest, the study of weightier matters seems to be quite logical. Now we are of course only suggesting a principle, the use of which rests with each individual.

One point worth noticing is, that at the end of the twenty minutes we may be tempted to extend it to thirty minutes. This is something we must overcome. If we have set ourselves on reading for only twenty minutes, we must read for only twenty minutes. And this will likewise prevent us from yielding to the temptation to sometimes shorten the period to ten minutes. Once we make a decision before God, let us discipline ourselves to keep it. Rather to do it for ten years than to forfeit it in ten days. Never be a careless and loose person, but learn to be scrupulously disciplined.

Second Section—The Study of Lighter Topics.

For the next twenty minutes, turn to something comparatively lighter such as the study of terminology. There are at least two to three hundred special terms which require study. For example, the term "blood" is used more than four hundred times in the Bible. Read all the places in the Scriptures where blood is mentioned, jotting down the more important verses and joining together verses with similar meaning, and thus will there be composed for ourselves a Bible reference which is much more meaningful than purchasing a reference Bible. And if we can memorize them, it is even better. In future days the Spirit of God may give us many revelations; and when a revelation does come, we can instantly correlate all the words in the entire Bible concerning this particular subject. Another term that can be studied is "calling". One brother once divided it into ten sections (see below, Plans for Bible Study No. 26). So we may use twenty minutes each day to study it also.

Keep in mind that it is quite enough to spend just twenty minutes daily to study terminology. Do not expect to finish studying one term all at once. Some terms have to be studied for at least two months. We must spent time and effort in reading the Bible. We should not be careless, lest what we have turns out to be not the Sword of the Holy Spirit but a reed that is totally useless.

For this reason we need to undertake a substantial study of the Bible. If our study is substantial, our preaching will also be substantial; by the same token, our preaching will be casual if our study is casual. Suppose someone tells us that in receiving the blood we may have new life. If we had carefully examined the term "blood" we would know such a presentation is erroneous; for the life in the blood is the soul life, not the new life. We therefore need to know the Bible teaching on all these basic truths, otherwise we shall simply follow whatever we are told and thus be misled. Yet to know these basic truths is not something accomplished in one day. Unless we study term after term, we will not know what the Bible teaches. Young brothers and sisters must diligently carry on this inquiry. If we can study two dozen terms each year, we will be able to cover almost all the main terms in both the Old and New Testaments in ten years.

Third Section—Collecting.

During the third section use ten minutes daily for the work of collecting. What is it to collect? One example is to consider the respective significance of all the metals in the Bible—gold, silver, copper, iron, and so forth. The precious stones in the Scriptures have their special meanings too. Let us not despise them as being too insignificant to be considered, for in the interpretation of the Bible these items are quite important. Why a *brazen* serpent? Why, in Revelation 1.15, does the passage say of the Lord that "his feet [were] like unto burnished brass, as if it had been refined in a furnace"? Why is the head of the terrible image, of which Nebuchadnezzar dreamed, of fine gold? Why must all the things in the temple be of fine gold? Why is the ark overlaid with gold and not with silver? Why are the sockets under the tabernacle made of silver? To what does the lead in Zechariah 5 point? All these require careful study before their meanings can be unveiled. So that during this third time segment let us collect these materials and list their corresponding verses one after another. These materials may be used in the future either during the first section for meditation or during the second section for light reading. In other words, the ten minutes of this third period are spent in gathering materials for the study done in either the first or the second period.

Yet another example of collecting can be cited. The Letter to the Ephesians mentions the Holy Spirit ten times. We may utilize the time during the third section to find out these ten places. Ephesians 1.13 speaks of being "sealed with the Holy Spirit". Let us collect all the places in the New Testament where the seal of the Holy Spirit is mentioned. Or in Ephesians 1.17 we read the phrase, "a spirit of wisdom and revelation". Take down every Scripture verse which has any bearing on the relation between the Spirit and wisdom. After we have collected and prepared all these materials, we may bring them to the first or the second section for study. Without these materials how can we be accurate in our study?

Fourth Section—Paraphrasing.
The fourth section, lasting ten minutes, is used for paraphrasing. Having obtained a new understanding of a passage, let us paraphrase it with easily understood words so that everybody may know the meaning. Through such an exercise we can readily see how every word in the Scriptures is exact and meaningful. The work of paraphrasing demands great care. Conceivably one verse of Scripture might require several days of paraphrasing without success. We need to touch the thought of the Holy Spirit with our spirit. We must open ourselves to the Word till we receive an impression before we attempt to rewrite. Our thought should follow closely the thought of the writer of the Bible passage; so also our words should be mainly in the words of the writer, only we add to them a little bit of our understanding so as to render them more easily to be grasped.

Paraphrase the Scriptures by sections. To do one verse is too short, to do a chapter is too long. The best is to combine a few verses as one unit. Read the whole section first, then paraphrase it verse by verse.

Paraphrase is neither a translation (which can be too simple and superficial) nor an exposition (which tends to be long and complicated). It may be said as standing between translation and exposition, possessing a little of each. Exposition is to explain the Bible in our own words, while paraphrase is to rewrite it with the words of the original writer. Translation is to put down the Scripture according to its original meaning, but in paraphrasing we may add a little of our own explanation. Hence paraphrase stands between translation and exposition. It adopts the tone of the original text of the Bible writer, though at some place our own explanation is added to it. Wherever the reader of the Bible finds difficulty in comprehending, there he may understand through our paraphrase. Let us illustrate with a few examples.

"Paul a servant of Jesus Christ" (Rom. 1.1). "Servant" may be written as "bondslave". Paul uses this term to show that as the Master's bondslave he is as one without his own freedom. Whether or not you want to explain the meaning of this term "servant" is a matter of your own personal preference. If you do desire to explain it, then you might conceivably write as follows: "I Paul, who was sold to sin and is now bought back by the blood of the Lord Jesus, have become a bondslave to Him." Thus written, any misunderstanding concerning both the Lord's right and our consecration will be avoided. I was originally sold to sin, but today He has redeemed me; so I gladly and willingly choose to serve Him. Due to His purchase and my choice, I now am His bondslave.

Further, from the phrase "called to be an apostle" to be found in this same verse, we may easily construe it to mean that Paul is called to be an apostle. In actual fact, though, this should be translated according to the original as simply "called an apostle". Not that he is called to be an apostle, but he is a called apostle. The same situation occurs in verse 7: "to all that are in Rome, beloved of God, called to be saints." The "to be" is again a problem. Some people may try to be such for a lifetime, and yet they still fail to be saints. However, according to the original this should be translated "called saints"—which means called as saints, not called to be saints. The word "called" here is an adjective and not a verb. It tells of the kind of apostle or saints. It explains a situation rather than expresses an action. One of the advantages in paraphrasing the Scriptures lies in discovering many Bible truths through words or phrases.

Similarly, "our old man was crucified with him" (Rom. 6.6) may be paraphrased in various ways. It may be written: "Since our old man was crucified with him, there is no need for us to be crucified again." Or if we wish to emphasize the point of how we can be co-crucified with Him, we may paraphrase it as: "Because God has put us in Christ, therefore we are crucified with Him." This paraphrase is based on Romans 6.11 which reads: "Even so reckon ye also yourselves to be dead unto sin . . . in Christ Jesus." On the basis of "in Him" we are "with Him". "With Him" follows "in Him". Without there being an "in Him" there can be no "with Him". Those who are not in Christ cannot be crucified with Him; only those who are "in Him" are crucified "with Him". Because God has put us in Christ, therefore we are crucified with Him.

The work of paraphrasing is to rewrite a passage more thoroughly. In each verse of the Bible there is an emphatic word which requires special attention. If we encounter any Scripture verse we do not understand, we should ask God to enlighten us that we may rewrite it in a form simpler than exposition and plainer than the original translation. Each time we paraphrase, let us think in this way: Why is this sentence difficult to comprehend? If we take care of the emphatic word first, then we will know how to rewrite the sentence. To illustrate: the word "crucified" in the Greek points to an accomplished fact. So that we may rewrite the sentence as: "Our crucifixion with Christ is an accomplished fact and not an experience to seek after." To be crucified is a personal experience to Christ himself, for *He* it is who was crucified. But as for me, there is no need for me to be individually crucified, because being in Him I was already crucified with Him. It has become a fact to me. The above indicates that this verse may be written in various ways, depending on the degree of personal understanding and a consideration for other people too. Whatever way it is paraphrased, it should be so written as to help the simple to understand.

Still another instance can be found: "And I, brethren, could not speak unto you as unto spiritual, but as unto carnal, as unto babes in Christ" (1 Cor. 3.1). The word "but" here is of special importance. It means, "You have believed the Lord for these many years; you ought to know what it is to be spiritual, to be under the control of the Holy Spirit. But due to the fact that you are influenced by the flesh in many things—working according to the flesh and not learning to be subject to the authority of the Holy Spirit—I am compelled to judge you as carnal." If the phrase "as unto babes in Christ" is followed out, Paul seems to have this thought: "You have extended the time too long. It is pardonable for beginners to be influenced by the flesh, but you have believed in the Lord these many years and yet you are still under the power of the flesh. Even today you are not yet grown up in Christ, and I have to feed you with milk, etc. etc." As a rule, you fill in what you have comprehended until you are satisfied with its clarity. And after you have thus paraphrased the entire letter of Paul to the Corinthians, spending ten minutes daily in rewriting it, you will at the end have a good understanding of the letter.

The above time arrangement is suggested on the basis

of the experience of a number of people. In applying it, let each consider his own practical situation and make a proper arrangement before God.

B. NOTE-TAKING.

In studying the Bible we should take notes as we read. Each reader of the Scriptures must learn to take notes. Always carry in the pocket a small notebook to record any question or good thought which may come at any time. Then prepare a large notebook for systematic entry of materials already considered and found. Such entry should be clearly classified so as to enhance any future research. As a start, do not classify materials too finely. If the theological approach is adopted, the classification may be composed of only five large items: Father, Son, the Spirit, the Church, the Future World. Typology concerning the church may be included in the item of the Church. Even all the teachings from justification to sanctification can very easily be placed under the same heading of the Church. Later on, when a far greater number of materials are prepared, more detailed classification may be required.

Notes should be taken carefully. For example, in Romans 5.14,17,21, the word "reign" is used four times; in Romans 5.9,10,15,17, the words "much more" are also used four times. These should be noted. Again, Mark 13.9 says "for my sake"; 13.13 says "for my name's sake"; and 13.20 says "for the elect's sake". Why are they put differently? Also, in Matthew 24 and 25, how many questions did the disciples put to the Lord on the Mount of Olives? How many verses are in answer to one question, and how many verses are in answer to the other question? The knowledge of the disciples was rather limited, and so their questions were few and inaccurate; but the Lord Jesus answered them with many words. Notice which passages constitute answers to their questions and which passages are words added on by the Lord himself. Thus shall we have a thorough understanding of the whole prophetic discourse on the Mount of Olives. Moreover, "I said" or "said I" is found three times in Isaiah 6.5,8,11. The first "said I" is confession; the second "I said" is consecration; and the third "said I" is communion. Things such as these should be noted down. For these materials are most useful both for ourselves and for other brothers and sisters. All who know how to study the Bible are diligent people; nothing is accomplished in this matter by chance.

C. INSTRUMENTS.

Studying the Bible is like doing any other work: it requires proper instruments.

Bible—Besides a pocket-size Bible for carrying to meetings, each person should have two regular-size Bibles for study. In the one Bible, notes may be inscribed, symbols may be inserted, and lines may be drawn. In the other Bible, nothing should be written or drawn. This latter is to prevent us from being influenced by the notes, symbols and lines we have set down before. For our daily spiritual food use the Bible without notes and signs; for doing research use the one with notes and drawings.

It will also be good to have a few different versions of the Bible for reference.

Concordance—Besides the Bible, get a good concordance.

Dictionary—A sound Bible dictionary proves to be

handy. For instance, to find the meaning of "urim and thummim" or the history of the six "Marys", we can be readily informed by consulting a Bible dictionary.

Outline Bible—Get an Outline Bible which gives a comparatively sound outline of each book of the Scriptures.

All these reference books are helps to the study of the Bible. They are necessary instruments.

3 | Plans for Bible Study

The Bible is a wonderful book. It includes sixty-six books—written by more than thirty-nine or forty authors—exceedingly rich in content. In studying it we need to have a plan, the lack of which deprives us of a good harvest. What follows here are twenty-eight different plans. If time permits us, we should work on all of them. For the older brethren, a few of the plans ought to be put into practice.

Plan 1   Principal Persons

There are a number of principal personalities in the Old Testament such as Adam, Abel, Abraham, Isaac, Jacob, Moses, Joshua, Daniel, and Solomon. We should make a detailed study of these lives, finding their histories not only in the Old but also in the New Testament.

Let us take as one example the history of Adam. We usually restrict the history of Adam to Genesis 2 and 3; but in searching the Bible carefully, we discover there are important references about Adam in Romans and 1 Corinthians. If we continue the search, we find Adam is also alluded to in Ephesians 5. In studying his history let us notice his place in the plan of God, how he was created, what kind of neutral or innocent life he possessed immediately after creation, what his relationship was with Eve, how God judged him after he had sinned and what promise was given to him, how he was driven out of the Garden of Eden, what kind of life he lived outside the Edenic garden, and finally how he was related to the last Adam. If we spend three or four months time in careful study, we will begin to understand some of the basic problems in the Bible.

After finishing the study of Adam, we may take up the history of Abel. Read about him in Hebrews 11 as well as in Genesis. Read all the places in the Scriptures connected with Abel. Learn what is the essential word God wishes to speak to us through this life. Why did God accept Abel and not Cain? Many people assume that the sacrifice of Abel was accepted by God simply because there was blood in the sacrifice. This tends to over-emphasize the New Testament interpretation, thus veiling the fundamental reason for the acceptance of his sacrifice. The work originally appointed for man in the Garden of Eden was to till and to guard. After man had sinned, it was quite proper for him to maintain his livelihood by farming (as was the case with Cain), but it was not proper for him to offer its produce to God. Why? Because man had sinned; and in offering the fruit of the field, Cain seemed to forget that man had sinned. This was why his offering was rejected. Suppose a child, after committing a serious offense, acts as if nothing has happened. Do you think his parents can accept him? God repudiates all who have sinned and yet are insensitive. The error of Cain lay in his lack of sensitivity towards the sin of man, whereas Abel acknowledged the fact of man having sinned. Now at that time shepherding was not for livelihood (for meat-eating began only after the flood; see Genesis 9.3). The only motive in tending a flock was for obtaining sacrifice. After a sheep was slain, its skin was good for clothing (see Gen. 3.21). God required but one thing of man, which was, that man must acknowledge his own sin. Abel came to God in accordance with God's demand, and therefore he was accepted by God.

We may continue on with the stories of Noah, Abraham, Isaac, Jacob, and so forth.

Plan 2 Women

In the Bible the women form a special line. They can be studied separately. Begin with Eve. See how she was made, what she said, how she acted independently, how she fell and the consequence, what promise God gave her, and how she became the mother of all living. Follow this up with a study of Sarah, Rebecca, Tamar, Ruth, Rahab, Hannah, Abigail, the Shunamite, and so on till you come to the woman with child in Revelation 12, the great harlot in Revelation 17, and the bride of the lamb in Revelation 19. Thus shall we notice a line that runs the entire way through. All these women in the Scriptures represent the various aspects of that woman which is the church, regardless whether the representation is negatively or positively presented.

Plan 3 Types

In order to study the types in the Old Testament it is necessary to have a good foundation in the New Testament. Four big spiritual topics are found in the New

Testament; namely, Christ, redemption, church, and the Holy Spirit. Accordingly, the principal types in the Old Testament are concerned with these four items. They typify either Christ or redemption or the church or the Holy Spirit. People during the Old Testament period beheld the "photos" before they knew the persons; but we during the New Testament period know the persons first and then look back at their pictures. We have already seen Christ, redemption, the church, and the Holy Spirit; so it is relatively easy for us now to retrospectively study Old Testament types.

In Genesis 1, for instance, the restoration is a type of the new creation. In Genesis 2 Eve represents the church without sin. Whenever we consider ourselves, we are reminded of sin. This is due to the deep-rooted relation between sin and us. Nevertheless, God shows us that the relationship between Christ and the church is beyond and above sin, for such relationship commenced at Genesis 2 and not at Genesis 3. The relationship between Adam and Eve began in Genesis 2, therefore theirs was outside of sin, just as the relationship between Christ and the church is beyond the realm of sin. Let us not link the thought of the church with that of sin, because in the eyes of God the church seems to be without sin. The Lord Jesus died for sinners in order to atone for sin, yet for the church He did not die for sin but did so to give life. In Genesis 3 there are the fig leaves and the coats of skin. In Genesis 4 there are offerings.

Further on, we read of Isaac. Who does Isaac typify? Is it the church or the Holy Spirit or redemption or the Lord Jesus? By our reading the New Testament it would seem he is more a type of the Lord Jesus. Isaac resembles the Lord Jesus in that so far as Isaac is concerned he is born through promise. He is his father's only begotten son in the eyes of Sarah. He receives everything from his father Abraham just as the Lord Jesus receives all from the Father. As God sends the Holy Spirit to earth to establish the church which is espoused to Christ to be in the future "the wife of the lamb", so Isaac's father sends the servant to his native land to find a woman out of his kindred—even Rebecca—to be Isaac's wife. By comparing these two sides point by point, many aspects of the type will be discovered.

If we read Galatians we find that Isaac also represents spiritual Christians. In the church there are the Ishmaels who represent the works of the flesh and there are the Isaacs who represent the works of the Holy Spirit. Ishmael is born of Abraham through Hagar, born of the flesh; therefore he stands for man's own works. Isaac, on the other hand, is born at a time when Abraham is beyond capability of begetting—being therefore born through promise; and so he stands for the works of the Holy Spirit. Among all the books of the Bible, Genesis ranks highest in typology. It may be said that Genesis is the seed plot of the whole Bible.

Exodus typifies being saved from the world. Passover foreshadows the breaking of bread, while crossing the Red Sea signifies baptism. The murmurings and the wanderings in the wilderness represent the various conditions of many of God's children today. The living water speaks of the Holy Spirit.

As for the tabernacle, it suggests our earthly path as well as that of our Lord Jesus on earth. The tabernacle has no floor, since it is a tent on the desert sand. It awaits the appearing of the New Jerusalem, the street of which is pure gold. While we pass through this world our fellowship with the Lord is glorious, but God wants us to enter into Canaan and not to remain in the desert.

Further on in the book of Numbers we observe that Israel passed through forty-two stations after they came out of Egypt and before they entered into Canaan. Every station has its spiritual significance. By studying these names of locality we will be shown the way to Canaan as well as man's history of wanderings.

We should also study carefully the offerings, the feasts, and the laws of cleansing in Leviticus—all of which are distinct types.

Move on to Joshua which is a profound book of typology. We do not suggest that every one of the types in Joshua is deep; we only maintain that in it are to be found many profound things. In order to understand how Israel entered Canaan and what battles the people fought in Canaan, we must first determine what Canaan represents. Some consider Canaan as a type of heaven. If so, will there still be fighting in heaven? If we study with care, though, we will discover that instead of being a type of heaven Canaan actually represents our present spiritual position. It is equal to "the heavenly places" in Ephesians. We are now seated with Christ in the heavenly places; meanwhile we are wrestling against the spiritual hosts of wickedness in the heavenly places (see Eph. 6.12).

All who study typology must read Ephesians as well as Joshua. Furthermore, Joshua must not only be studied with that book but also with Hebrews. For the entering of Canaan in Joshua serves as a double type: on the one hand it typifies spiritual warfare, and thus is connected with Ephesians; on the other hand it signifies rest, which is therefore linked with Hebrews. The rest in Joshua points not to heaven, but to the Sabbath rest in the kingdom. Not all who were under the blood of the lamb entered Canaan, neither did all who ate the meat of the lamb enter therein. Only two men finally got into Canaan; the carcasses of all the rest fell in the wilderness. Many are called, but few are chosen. For this reason, Canaan also represents the kingdom. The entry into Canaan presents to us a type as to who are able to reign in the kingdom. If we can settle this basic problem, we will have no difficulty in distinguishing which part in Joshua typifies our present spiritual position and which part signifies our future reward.

The many unlawful things in the book of Judges forecasts the many confusions when every man does what is right in his own eyes.

In the books of Samuel we are given to see how man reigns and how God gives authority to man. Before the man after God's own heart came, the man after man's own heart first appeared. David was the man after God's heart, but Saul as the man after the people's heart preceded him to the throne. It is quite clear that Saul is a type of the Antichrist who reigns. We are also shown how the king whom God has chosen went to war and enjoyed peace. There were the wars of David but also the glory of Solomon; there were the Saul in tribulation, the David after tribulation, and the Solomon of the millennial kingdom. All these are clear types.

Moreover, in the books of Kings the building of the temple by Solomon typifies the building of the church by Christ. Just as the holy temple was in Jerusalem, so the church which the temple signifies gathers and worships in the Lord's name. For God's name was placed in Jerusalem; it was the only place where God was recognized and where He chose to set His name (see 1 Kings 14.21). When Jeroboam rose up to be a king over the separated kingdom of Israel, he set up altars as places of worship in Bethel and Dan. His action was condemned by God, because God was only pleased with worship in the place where His name was set and not in any other place. During times of revival some kings rose up to destroy these altars, but some kings did not destroy the altars. This serves as a shadow of the various conditions during revival times in church history. Afterwards the temple was destroyed, which action is a type of the ruin of the church. Eventually, as we see in the later historical books of the Old Testament, Ezra, Nehemiah, Zechariah, Zerubbabel and others returned to rebuild the temple and the city. Though the restoration never reached the former glory, it nevertheless began to be recovered to the original position. This typifies the recovery of the church which shall be consummated at the return of the Lord. Then shall the church become a glorious church.

Plan 4 Prophecy

One third of the entire Bible is prophecy. We can divide its prophecy into two classes: that which concerns the first coming of the Lord Jesus and that which relates to His second coming. In the Pentateuch, in Psalms, and in the Prophets there are prophecies about the first coming of the Lord Jesus. Some may not be interested in such prophecies, since the Lord Jesus has already come. But if we wish to study prophecy we must pay attention to His first coming. We should find all the places in the Old and the New Testaments concerning the first coming of the Lord Jesus, and write them down. But what is the use of it? It can help us to discover the principle regarding fulfillment of prophecy. In the manner in which the prophecies of the Lord's first coming were fulfilled, in just such a manner shall all the prophecies about His second coming be fulfilled.

The Scriptures have a definite rule towards the explanation of each and every thing. Whenever there is the need of spiritualizing, the Bible itself usually points it out. For instance, the "seven stars" seen by John in the right hand of the Lord as recorded in Revelation 1 refer, as it plainly says there, to "the angels of the seven churches." This is not a literal interpretation, and the Scripture itself tells us so. The Lord walks among the seven golden candlesticks which allude to the seven churches. This too is shown us in the very text itself. Naturally types should be spiritualized, such as Adam points not to Adam but to Christ; and Eve, not to Eve but to the church. But the interpretation of prophecy has two basic principles: one is to interpret prophecy according to its spiritual meaning, and hence it has reference to an implied fulfillment; the other principle is to interpret prophecy according to its letter, thus referring to a literal fulfillment. Let us illustrate this in the words of Matthew 2.17,18: "Then was fulfilled that which was spoken through Jeremiah the prophet, saying, A voice was heard in Ramah, weeping and great mourning, Rachel weeping for her children; and she would not be comforted, because they were not." This is an implied fulfillment. Also, "This is that which hath been spoken through the prophet Joel" (Acts 2.16) means the situation today is similar to that of which Joel had spoken much earlier. So that it is an implied fulfillment. As regards the first coming of the Lord Jesus, many prophecies are fulfilled in a very literal way. A virgin is a virgin, Egypt is Egypt, not a bone is broken is not a bone broken. All these are fulfilled quite literally. Since many of the prophecies concerning our Lord's first coming are literally fulfilled, the prophecies of His second coming will likewise mainly be literally fulfilled.

There are prophecies concerning the Jews, the Gentiles, and the church. These three kinds are different one from another. The prophecies concerning the Jews are found mostly in Moses and Balaam, and of course in the books of the Prophets. Furthermore, the prophecies concerning the Jews may be subdivided into two branches: namely, that which is related to the day of the Lord and that which is related to the earthly blessings during the millennium. Concerning the prophecies of the Gentiles, special attention should be given to the Book of Daniel, to the words of the Lord Jesus in Matthew 24, and to Revelation 8-11, 13, 15, 16 and 18. The prophecies concerning the church can be seen in Matthew 13, Revelation 2, 3, 12, 14 and 15, 1 Corinthians 15, and 1 Thessalonians 4. We need to distinguish these three kinds of prophecies.

As to the prophecies concerning the Gentiles, we should pay attention to all God's prophecies surrounding the time of the Gentiles after the fall of the Jewish nation. Scriptures such as Daniel 2, 4, 7, and the "seventy sevens" of Chapter 9 and on to Revelation are all prophecies concerning the Gentiles. In brief, the first stage begins from the fall of the Jewish nation to the time of the end. This is especially foretold in the history of the huge image in Daniel 2. The second stage concerns the ten horns at the time of the end and another little horn—ten kings and another king, even the Antichrist. The third stage deals with the blessings of the Gentiles during the millennium.

The prophecies of the church are in regard to: first, the two thousand year history of the church; second, the rapture; third, the judgment seat of Christ; fourth, the kingdom; and fifth, eternity.

Plan 5 Dispensation

The dealings of God with man vary according to different dispensations. In each dispensation God has a distinctive way. He treats people one way in one dispensation and another way in another dispensation. His demand on people's conduct in one period is also unlike that of another period. The way to salvation in one dispensation likewise varies from that of the other dispensation. If we are not clear on dispensational truth, we may feel confused as to the word of the Bible. Once we are able to plainly identify the dispensations, we will no longer be perplexed.

With respect to the demarcation of these periods, some commentators divide the time into seven dispensations, though according to the Bible itself it falls naturally into four periods. The first dispensation is that of the fathers. When does it commence? It begins with Adam, since there is the clear statement in Romans 5.14: "From Adam until Moses". Though there are many deviations, these are all rather minor; hence it is still "from Adam until Moses". The second is the dispensation of law. It extends from Moses until Christ. Why does it extend until Christ? Because the Lord Jesus had declared: "All the prophets and the law prophesied until John [Baptist]" (Matt. 11.13; see also Luke 16.16). The third is the dispensation of grace which stretches from the first coming of Christ to His second coming (see Acts 15.14-18). Although the Lord is still mindful of the Jews, the center of His attention has shifted to the Gentiles, for the dispensation of grace has already begun. The fourth is the dispensation of the kingdom. It covers the period from the second coming of Christ until the end of the kingdom (see Rev. 20).

Let us notice in each dispensation the original place of

man, his responsibility, his failure, and God's dealing with him. By studying these matters carefully, we will solve all the apparent contradictions in the Bible.

Plan 6 Topics

The Bible contains numerous topics, such as creation, man, angels, sin, satanic kingdom, salvation, repentance, the person of Christ, the work of Christ, the life of Christ, the Holy Spirit, regeneration, eternal life, eternal security, sanctification, justification, election, forgiveness, righteousness, deliverance, the law, revelation, inspiration, the body of Christ, the ministry of God's word, the authority of God, the second coming of the Lord, judgment, the kingdom, eternity, and so forth. At the beginning, study a topic each year. Later on, this may be increased to two or to four topics a year.

Take the person of Christ as an illustration. This is a most comprehensive subject. How should one go about it? It may be divided into the following areas: (1) He is God. There is "the Word" aspect as well as "the Son of God" aspect. (2) He becomes man, that is, how He becomes Jesus and how He expresses himself as man. (3) He is God and man. In sleeping in the stern of a boat, He reveals himself as man; in rising up to calm the sea, though, He manifests himself as God. By attending the wedding feast, He shows His humanity; but in changing water into wine, He demonstrates His divinity. In asking water from the Samaritan woman He shows He is human, while in explaining the living water to that woman He unveils His deity. (4) His history, that is, His life on earth. (5) His present position, which is His place after ascension. (6) His future position, that is, His glorious place at His return.

Or in studying the work of Christ, we may use the following division: (1) the relation between the person and the work, (2) the substitutionary work of the Lord, (3) the redemption that satisfies God, (4) reconciliation of God and men, (5) His acceptance of men, (6) His priestly ministry, and (7) His mediatorial work.

Now the life of Christ can be divided into: (1) birth, (2) death, (3) resurrection, (4) ascension, and (5) second coming. As regards birth, we need to understand what it means. By looking at all the consequences of His birth, we may define it as the substantiating of all that is abstract and the humanizing of all that is of God. For example, we talk about the patience of God. What is the patience of God? We not only know nothing about it; we just cannot know it. Yet, the Lord Jesus is born; the Word is become flesh. And so, it is patience made flesh. That abstract, invisible thing called patience is now being substantiated into something concrete and practical. The principle of incarnation is to show us how love has become flesh, how holiness has become flesh, how joy has become flesh, how obedience has become flesh, etc. In other words, all the virtues of God which are essentially inapprehensible have now turned into things apprehensible indeed. God has become man, the abstract is now made concrete. The model man whom God looks for is this Jesus. We are unable to approach God because we fall short of God's standard. The veil hangs between. The more attractive the veil, the less able we can draw near.

But thank God, there is His death. What is the meaning of death? On the one hand, His death is redemption; on the other hand, it terminates all that is of the old creation. The death of Christ is the termination of all things. The veil being rent from top to bottom speaks of death.

Yet there is also His resurrection. It is a new beginning, God's creative power, a new life which cannot be
held by death. Death is unable to confine life and block its
exit. Death does not possess such power. Resurrection
proves its strength by passing through trial and death.

Furthermore, there is also His ascension, which puts
Satan under us. Christ's ascension places us in the same
position as His, that we may enjoy His victory.

But then there is the second coming of the Lord, which
is the manifestation of a new authority.

To sum up, then, birth speaks of God's standard;
death speaks of the termination of the old creation which
is below par; resurrection speaks of a new beginning;
ascension, of a new position; and second coming, of a
glorious manifestation. How precious are all these in the
sight of God.

Plan 7 Relationship between God and Man

Concerning the relationship between God and man,
some make the following divisions: (1) God, (2) men
(referring to mankind), (3) individual man, (4) God and
man, (5) man with God, (6) God among men, and (7) God
above men. Such divisions are quite good.

The first point "God" is clear enough. The second
point "men" refers to mankind. It includes Adam and his
sin and all those who are in Adam. The third point
"individual man" consists of personal sin and personal
penalty. The fourth point "God and man" is recorded in
the Gospels, for the Lord Jesus is both God and man. The
fifth point "man with God" is related to the truth of the
gospel as preached in the Epistles. The sixth point "God
among men" speaks of all the operations of God in men,

which form the deeper part of the Epistles. And the seventh point "God above men" points to the kingdom age when God shall reign over all. Hence all future events are included in it.

Plan 8 Chronology

Although the study of Biblical chronology does not have too much usefulness, it nonetheless helps people to cultivate the habit of a careful study of the Word. Biblical chronology is very clear. The years from the creation of man to the birth of the Lord Jesus can be computed. From Adam to the flood (Noah) there are 1656 years. The duration of the history of the Exodus up through the entry and conquest of Canaan, the duration of the histories of the judges, of the kings, of Daniel, and on up to Christ can all be found in the Bible. Some must be learned from the words of Stephen, others may be counted from the years Ezekiel lay upon the left side and the right side of his body (Ez. 4.4-6). Between the rebuilding of Jerusalem to the Lord Jesus there are sixty-nine sevens (483 years), which should also be added. Thus the years from Adam to Christ are all accountable. Commencing with the book of Genesis, it seems as if God is offering a chronological chart uninterrupted.

In studying Biblical chronology we may discover what we usually miss. For instance, if we compute the time of the early history we know that when Enoch was on earth Adam was still living. Adam had seen God, but Enoch had not seen Him. To our natural mind, if a man is to be raptured it should be the one who has seen God. Yet instead of Adam, Enoch was the one raptured. This can teach us a lesson. Further on, we notice that the name

Methuselah means "when he dies something will happen". It so happened that at the death of Methuselah the flood came. How accurate the Bible is.

Moreover, Paul shows us in Galatians 3 that grace precedes, not follows, law; for the grace of promise had been preached for four hundred thirty years before the law came.

No doubt Biblical chronology is easy to trace in Genesis. It is not quite as easy afterwards. The problem actually lies in our failure to find it. For example, how many years were there from the exodus of the children of Israel to the building of the temple by Solomon? 1 Kings 6.1 records: "And it came to pass in the four hundred and eightieth year after the children of Israel were come out of the land of Egypt, in the fourth year of Solomon's reign over Israel, in the month Ziv, which is the second month, that he began to build the house of Jehovah." But Acts 13.18-22 states, "And for about the time of forty years as a nursing-father bare he them in the wilderness . . . He gave them their land for an inheritance, for about four hundred and fifty years: and after these things he gave them judges until Samuel the prophet. And afterward . . . Saul . . . for the space of forty years. And when he had removed him, he raised up David to be their king." By adding these years together, we have a number of five hundred thirty years. Add further the forty years of David's reign (1 Kings 2.11) and the three years of Solomon before he started building the temple, and we come to a total number of 573 years. So that the number of years given in 1 Kings 6 is 93 years less than that shown in Acts 13.

Why is there such a discrepancy? According to the record of the book of Judges, the children of Israel were under foreign rule five times: eight years during the first time (3.8), 18 years the second time (3.14), 20 years the third time (4.2-3), seven years the fourth time (6.1), and 40 years the fifth time (13.1). They add up to exactly 93 years. Though the record in 1 Kings would appear to have missed 93 years, in actuality it purposely discounts the years under foreign domination. We need to take what is written in Judges and insert them in 1 Kings. The words of the Bible are like a chain of rings; none is missing; each one links up with the other. God has already put these rings in the Bible; all we must do is to find them. Hence the study of Biblical chronology is quite useful in training our accuracy.

Plan 9   Numbers

The numbers in the Bible have their respective meanings.

"One" is the number of the one and only God.

"Two" is the number of fellowship.

"Three" is God's number, for God is a triune God. "One" points to the unity of God, whereas "three" points to the completion or perfection of God.

"Four" is the first number after "three". By adding "one" to "three" we have this number "four". So that it is the number of the created. All that is related to the created things is in "four": such as four corners of the earth, four seasons of the year, four winds of the earth, four heads of the river that flows from the Garden of Eden, the four parts of the image seen in Nebuchadnezzar's dream, the four beasts coming out of the sea, and the four living creatures which represent the whole creation. Then too, we have the four Gospels to present us with the earthly life of the Lord Jesus. Consequently, what emerges after God is the number "four".

"Five" is man's differential number, such as five fingers

on each of two hands, and five wise and five foolish of the ten virgins. "Five" is also the number of man's responsibility before God. In view of the ear being one of the five organs, the thumb one of the five fingers, and the great toe one of the five toes, the blood is applied on man's right ear, right thumb and right great toe. This indicates how man is separated to bear responsibility before God.

"Six" is the number of man. For man is created on the sixth day of creation. "Six" falls short of "seven" which is the number of perfection. Whatever man does cannot be compared with what God does.

"Seven" is the number of perfection, though it is today's temporary perfection rather than the permanent perfection in eternity. As "three" is God's number and "four" is the number of creation, so the coming together of the Creator and the creation makes up perfection. But this is the *adding* of "four" and "three", so that its perfection is of a temporary nature. The Bible as a rule uses the number "seven" to represent all temporary perfections, such as seven days in a week, seven parables in Matthew 13, and seven churches, seven candlesticks, seven angels, seven seals, seven trumpets, seven bowls in the book of Revelation. All these are temporary, not eternal perfections.

"Eight" is the number of resurrection, for "seven" denotes a period or span of time, while "eight" is the first number after "seven". Our Lord Jesus is resurrected on the eighth day; consequently, "eight" is the number of resurrection.

"Nine" is "three" times "three", hence it is a reinforced number of God. This means that the testimony of God is not only God's word but also God's word to us.

"Ten" is the number of man's perfection. When man's

number reaches ten, it is considered complete. Thus, we
have ten fingers to our hands and ten toes to our feet.

"Eleven" does not have any significance in Scripture.

"Twelve" is also the number of perfection, but it is
perfection in eternity. So that there are two numbers of
perfection: one of them is "seven", the other is "twelve".
"Seven" is a perfection that belongs to God, yet it is
today's perfection. "Twelve" too is God's perfection, but it
refers to eternal perfection. One fact seems strange, that
during the time of the new heaven and the new earth, the
number "seven" no longer exists. In the New Jerusalem
there are twelve gates, twelve foundations, the names of
the twelve apostles, twelve precious stones, and twelve
pearls; and the wall of the city is 144 cubits, which is
twelve multiplied by twelve. All these shall exist eternally,
hence the number "twelve" represents eternal perfection.
Why is it that "seven" is temporary perfection but
"twelve" is eternal perfection? Because three plus four is
merely the coming together of God and man. It is the
addition of the creation to the Creator. But three times four
is the *multiplication* of the Creator with the creation which
means the union of the two. "Multiplication" is different
from "addition" since the former causes a fusion of the
creation and the Creator which cannot be separated. Such
union is eternal. Therefore "twelve" represents eternal
perfection.

Plan 10 Parables

We should study all the parables in the Bible. And
upon reading several of the parables, we shall become
aware of the fact that the interpretation of parables
follows its definite rule and ought not to be explained at

will. Now if we are able to discover this rule, we will know how to interpret any new parable that comes to us.

In any parable there is a difference between the principal and the subordinate. We need to distinguish the principal lesson from the subordinate lesson in a parable. The passage touching the principal lesson must be explained point by point, whereas the subordinate part may be so explained or simply passed over. For instance, of the seven parables spoken by the Lord Jesus in Matthew 13, the first one is the parable of the sower: one kind of seed but four different kinds of ground—hence one seed but four different kinds of heart. Now this is the principal part. We should lay hold of this seed and all these different kinds of heart. Other fragmentary problems such as the "devouring" of the birds and the "fold" of a hundred, sixty and thirty in yield are not principal parts. We will be led off into tangents if we are attracted to the size and flying habit of these birds or the multiple of the yields. Therefore, in interpreting a parable the principal and the subordinate must first be distinguished.

Another matter to be noted is that no parable should be literally interpreted. The "sower" in the parable of the sower is not really a farmer who sows, neither is the "field" a real field, nor is the "seed" a real seed. It is absolutely certain that all parables have their respective spiritual meaning, and therefore they should be interpreted spiritually. This, however, does not imply that every point in a parable must be spiritually interpreted. Only the principal must be, whereas the subordinate part can be literally interpreted. Many make the mistake of attempting to spiritualize the subordinate after they have spiritually interpreted the principal. Matthew 13 records the first occasion of our Lord speaking in parables. The first of these parables is explained to us by the Lord himself. He has not explained each and every point; some of it He explains, some He does not. The parable of the sower can serve to illustrate this. Concerning the "good ground", the "ground" here points to the human heart, and the "good" to that which is honest and good. Since the Lord himself explains these to us, we now know that the principal thought is an honest and good heart. He does not explain to us later concerning the "fruit", hence we understand that it is not the principal. Interpreting with too much detail curtails its spiritual value and leads people astray. As it is not an easy task to interpret parables, we need to seek God's light on every one of them in order to give each of them its proper explanation.

Plan 11 Miracles

Pay special attention to the miracles performed by the Lord Jesus. Miracles done by Elijah and Elisha in the Old Testament and by Paul in the New Testament may also be studied. As we make this special study of the miracles, we will soon see that all these miracles have their characteristics. For example, the healing of the blind and the healing of the palsy are different. Eye is a matter of seeing clearly—the blind needs to see. Sick with palsy is a question of strength—the palsied needs to walk. In studying, first find out the characteristics peculiar to each, then notice how the Lord deals with each of their problems, which finally will indicate the way He deals with our problems spiritually.

In some miracles the Lord distinctively accompanies them with spiritual teachings, such as in the case of His healing the man born blind recorded in John 9. He plainly states there that "for judgment came I into this world, that they that see not may see; and that they that see may become blind" (v.39). Or in the instance of the raising from the dead of Lazarus found in John 11, the Lord plainly asserts: "I am the resurrection and the life."

In other miracles, although the Lord has not especially mentioned any teaching, there still must be inherent lessons there for us. How we need to go to God and seek for their meanings. As an example, take the case of the healing of the man sick of the palsy. When the Lord heals him He says to him, "Son, be of good cheer; thy sins are forgiven." Afterwards He also speaks and says, "Arise, and take up thy bed, and go unto thy house." And the man arose and departed to his house right before the crowd (Matt. 9.2,6). The spiritual principle involved is this: Besides the forgiveness of sin, there needs to be the manifestation of life and of a spiritual walk. No one can say he has received forgiveness of sin without rising up and walking. Having received forgiveness, there must be the ability to walk. Forgiveness preceeds walking, but walking is the result of forgiveness. What a vivid picture this is.

Plan 12 The Lord's Teaching on Earth

Read all the teachings of the Lord. Read carefully from Matthew 5, 6 and 7 through 13, 24 and 25. Much of the Lord's teaching may be found in Luke's Gospel and in John's Gospel. A passage such as John 14-16 is very important. In studying, notice when the Lord Jesus speaks. Also, where does He speak—in Judea or in Galilee? To whom does He speak—to the disciples or to the crowd, to the crowd as well as to the disciples, or to the disciples alone and not to the crowd? By studying in this manner we may be able to get the main teachings of the

New Testament. If we are called to do the Lord's work, we should at least study well the parables, the miracles, and the teachings of our Lord; else we have no material in our hands and will thus be unable to meet the outside need.

Plan 13 Comparing the Four Gospels

Comparing the Gospels is likewise a significant way of study. Why does the Holy Spirit write four different Gospels instead of one complete Gospel? Why do the narratives seem to be different, why are the orders of the narratives varied, and why are the numbers not identical? Without such a careful study, we shall fail to appreciate the wonder of the Holy Spirit's inspiration. By comparing these four Gospels we shall see a great number of dissimilarities, and all of them so arranged by the Holy Spirit.

Matthew, Mark, and Luke emphasize the work of the Lord Jesus in Galilee, while John emphasizes His work in Judea. This explains why the three synoptic Gospels are distinct from the last one. The stories, the teachings, as well as the miracles are different. There is a difference even between Mark and Luke, because the first stresses the deeds of the Lord Jesus while the second, the teachings of the Lord. Matthew, though, is balanced on both deeds and teachings.

Matthew sets down his record according to dispensational teaching, not according to chronological order. In other words, all the works of the Lord Jesus have dispensational significance. Some events occur this year, others two years later. But if their dispensational significance is the same, Matthew gathers them together. Such dispensational significance as regards the Jews and the

Gentiles cannot be found in Mark, nor can it be found in Luke and John. This is found only in Matthew. Passages such as Matthew 12 and 13 indicate a great divide, yet they are not in Mark, Luke, and John because these Gospels give no dispensational teaching. Keep well in mind that Matthew's narrative follows the order of dispensation, that is, how the Lord shows grace to the Jews and preaches the gospel among them, and how He subsequently turns to the church after being rejected by the Jews. If we wish to follow the chronological order of the miracles performed by the Lord, we should read Mark. For the order of teaching, read Luke. For the Lord's teaching in Judea, read John. And for the basic principles governing the teaching of the Lord Jesus and their dispensational significance, read Matthew.

Matthew presents the Lord Jesus as king, Mark as the servant, Luke as man, and John as the Son of God. The approach of each of these four Gospels is quite different.

All four Gospels speak of the coming of the Lord, but their ways of delineating this are varied. Matthew says, "Behold, thy King cometh unto thee" (21.5); Mark says, "The Son of man . . . came . . . to minister" (10.45); Luke says, "The Son of man came to seek and to save" (19.10); and John says He "came that they may have life"(10.10). Divergent emphases such as these are many in the Gospels. If we take time to study them, we shall readily see the characteristic of each Gospel.

Matthew 1 records the genealogy of the Lord Jesus, but so does Luke 3. The book of the generation of Jesus Christ in Matthew 1 is divided into three sections of fourteen generations each—from Abraham to David, from David to the carrying away to Babylon, and from the carrying away to Babylon to Christ. The genealogy in Luke, however, traces backward. While Matthew runs from Abraham to David, Luke runs from David back to Abraham. Matthew reads forward from David to the captivity, but Luke reads backward from Shealtiel to David. Matthew commences from Abraham, yet Luke traces from Abraham to Adam. If the genealogy in Matthew is divided into three sections, that of Luke will be four sections. The first section in Luke's genealogy is that of Mary's, and the last section of Matthew's genealogy is that of Joseph's. These sections must be clearly divided. In the study of the four Gospels, the first thing to do is to divide them into sections. We may prepare a large notebook and list the four Gospels in four columns so that we can observe their similarities and differences by comparing them.

Since Matthew presents the Lord Jesus as king, he points out especially in the genealogy that He is the son of David. Luke exhibits the Lord Jesus as man, and therefore his genealogy commences with Adam. As Mark presents the Lord Jesus as servant and John testifies of Him as the Son of God, neither of them gives any genealogy. Such comparison proves beyond doubt that indeed Matthew presents the Lord Jesus as king, Mark as servant, Luke as man, and John as the Son of God.

This kind of study does not give us revelation; it simply prepares the material. But when revelation does come, such material then becomes highly usable. In preaching, we need material as well as revelation; otherwise there will be no content. Hence we need preparation in our daily life.

We may purchase a copy of a large-letter single Gospel. First divide Matthew into five or ten sections. Study the book section by section, compare with the other three Gospels, collect and jot down the similarities and differences. Subdivide the sections: finer subdividing for similar sections and rougher subdividing for differing sections. As an example, take the parable of the sower which is in Matthew and is also found in Luke. Now subdivide it carefully and seek to discover the things which differ. Study to such degree that all the differences and similarities between them can easily be seen. Such study obviously requires much time. It takes at least two years to study the four Gospels.

Plan 14 Great Chapters

There are a number of important chapters in the Bible such as Genesis 2, 3, Numbers 21, and Deuteronomy 8. Psalm 22 and Isaiah 53 are equally very great chapters because they find more fulfillments in the New Testament. Daniel 9 is a great chapter too. Of the New Testament, Matthew 5-7, 13, 24 and 25 are all great chapters; so are John 14-16 and I Corinthians 13. There are probably thirty to forty such great chapters in the entire Bible, all needing to be rightly understood.

Plan 15 Past, Present, Future

This is a very simple way of study. Put all the past, present, and future things in the New Testament under their respective columns and study them one by one.

Things like all the earthly words of Christ, the coming of the Holy Spirit, and the beginning of the church belong to the past column; the intercessory work of the Lord, His mediatorship, the ministry of the church, the discipline of the Holy Spirit, the indwelling of the Holy Spirit, and the means of grace (In some places of Scripture, grace is given directly; while in other places God uses other means to dispense grace to us. Means such as the assembling together of the saints, the breaking of bread, baptism, laying on of hands, and so forth are called means of grace because through these means God dispenses grace to us.) are things of the present; resurrection, rapture, redemption of the body, glorification, and God's new creation pertain to the future. Although redemption is a thing of the past, it has not yet passed completely out of the picture, since it still waits to be fully realized at the redemption of the body. Unless the problem of the physical body has been solved, redemption is not yet complete. The redemptive work of the Lord Jesus on the cross lays the foundation, but its completion awaits the redemption of the body. We must clearly distinguish what things have already been done, what things are now being done, and what things are yet to be done by God.

Plan 16 Salvation, Holiness, and Ministry

Salvation refers to our receiving life; holiness pertains to our daily living; and ministry refers to our work. Whatever is related to the Lord's calling, the Lord's blood, the Lord's work, etc., may be put under the classification of salvation. All the works of the Holy Spirit may be classified under holiness. Things pertaining to faithfulness, testimony, and power of the Holy Spirit can all be placed under ministry. The cross of the Lord may also be listed under salvation; our cross, under holiness; and "the dying of Jesus" (or "the slaying of Jesus") mentioned in 2 Corinthians 4, under ministry. Locate our faith in salvation, our obedience in holiness, and our faithfulness in ministry. The life-giving of the Holy Spirit is salvation, the work of the Holy Spirit is holiness, and the power of the Holy Spirit is ministry. We can use three prepositions to represent them: "for" us, "in" us, and "through" us. All that is for us belongs to salvation; that which is in us belongs to holiness; and whatever is through us, to ministry. What is done for us is called salvation; what is done in us is holiness; and what is done through us is ministry or service. If we can distinguish these three aspects clearly, we shall be able to set all the teachings of the Bible in order.

Unfortunately many are quite confused about "God for us" and "God in us". For instance, "Christ crucified" and "we are crucified with Christ" are matters applied to "God for us", yet they are misinterpreted by the Roman church as being "God in us". This is decidedly erroneous. Where does the cross begin to be "in us"? It begins with *our* cross. It is a bearing the cross, not a crucifying on the cross. Bearing is ours while crucifying is the Lord's. This too explains the difference between the Roman church and the true Christian church. The "co-death" in the Scriptures is a matter of "for us", not "in us". Romans 6 is co-death; Romans 8 is putting to death; 2 Corinthians 4 is slaying. Hence Romans 6 belongs to salvation; Romans 8, to holiness; and 2 Corinthians 4, to ministry. We must be perfectly clear before God: "co-death" pertains exclusively to salvation, for it is the work of the Lord which we have entered into; the "putting to death" by the cross is our own affair; while the "slaying" is allowing the Holy Spirit to break forth through us and is consequently something of ministry. Do not consider this as being too elementary. Many are still unclear on "co-death" and "putting to death". The fact of "co-death" is not in *us,* but in *Christ.* Whatever is in Christ belongs to salvation; all that is in us is related to holiness; and all that comes out from us, pertains to ministry. These constitute a basic knowledge of the word of God which we must have.

Plan 17 Metals and Minerals

Each of the metals and minerals in the Bible possesses its respective significance. We should spend some time in studying them. We are not thereby suggesting that there are revelations in these things; we merely state that when God gives revelation He can speak to us through these materials. We need to store up within ourselves a reservoir of Scripture materials for ready use.

Gold, for example, represents the glory of God. Whatever is wholly of God is signified by gold. Silver stands for the redemption of the Lord. The Bible rarely if ever mentions the purchase of anything with gold, but always with silver. For silver expresses redemption. In other words, gold represents the Person of God; while silver, the work of God. Gold speaks of His glory, and silver of His redemption. Copper suggests judgment; iron, the authority of man, and lead, sin.

Moreover, the foundation of the wall of New Jerusalem is adorned with all manner of precious stones, among which is emerald. The color of emerald is green, which is a basic color—that of earthly life. It points especially to the work of the Holy Spirit. When we are studying metals and minerals, we need to examine their colors as well as their substance. Red is different from scarlet in spiritual application. Red points to the blood, but scarlet points to sin. The colors white, black, and purple all have their distinctive meanings. Let us classify them and search out their significance.

Plan 18 Geography

Mention is made in the Bible of many nations, cities, mountains, rivers, wells, and so forth; all of which possess meanings. Nations such as Assyria, Egypt, Babylon, Greece, and Persia; and cities like Samaria, Jerusalem, Caesarea, Sodom, Gomorrah, Babel, Ur, Shechem, Bethel, Mahanaim, and Gilgal—all have their respective significa- tion. Some of their meanings can be derived from the words themselves, while the implications of others can be deduced through their history. Bethel means the house of God; its meaning comes from the word itself. Gilgal typifies the cutting away of the flesh; its signification is learned from its history. Shechem means shoulder, so it carries the thought of responsibility or burden, and thus its meaning comes from the word itself. When Joshua divided the land, many cities were mentioned. They all reflect spiritual ideas which we need to ferret out. While the meanings of many words need to be looked up in a Hebrew dictionary, a number of them are explained right in the Bible. And hence we are still able to find out quite a number of their meanings even if we do not know Hebrew.

Mountains such as Sinai, Horeb, Lebanon, Pisgah, Olive, and so forth have their individual importance. Since Mount Horeb is Mount Sinai, why is it that sometimes it is called Mount Horeb and sometimes Mount Sinai? Let us find out the reason. Besides the mountains there are various valleys, such as the valley of Hinnom, the valley of Jehoshaphat, etc. There are rivers too, like the river of Egypt, the Jordan river, the River Euphrates, etc.

The meanings of geographic places, as we have said, can be derived from two sources: some from the words themselves, and some from history. But Calvary finds its significance both in word and in history, for Calvary is Golgotha which means place of a skull, and it is also the cross—an historical event. The River Euphrates also obtains its significance by word and by history. History tells us that the attack on Jerusalem came from the river

Euphrates, but the book of Revelation too predicts it. Consequently, it represents the authority and power of rebellion. Philistia likewise stands for the Satanic power of darkness, but its typology is deduced from history and not from word. Another place called Shiloh is exceedingly important because the problem regarding the church is to be learned there.

Much can be included in geography. If all the geographic places are carefully studied, they will serve a good and useful purpose in the future. But only the more important things need to be studied. Do not spend too much time on it; perhaps three or four months should be enough.

Plan 19   Personal Names

The Bible contains many personal names; and the meanings of the principal persons are also given in the Bible. It is of course better to have a Greek lexicon. The meanings of Adam, Eve, Cain, Seth, Abel, Noah, Melchizedek, Abraham, Sarah, Isaac, Jacob, Israel, Moses, Joshua, Samuel, David, Solomon, Micah, Zechariah, Peter, and others can easily be found. Moreover, such material should be gathered in ordinary days.

Plan 20   Chorus

In the Scriptures we sometimes find a sudden change in style of writing, a departure from that of the main text which is prose to the use of a type approaching poetry. Such a departure usually occurs within a few sentences, not within a large section. Hence we call this temporary or brief lapse into poetry a "chorus". This will be discovered by those who are well acquainted with Greek. The structure of such a change is similar to that of songs. Passages such as 1 Timothy 1.15, 3.15,16; Titus 3.4-8; Romans 10.8-10; 2 Timothy 2.11,13; Ephesians 4.8-9, 5.16; and 1 Thessalonians 4.14-17 are all in the form of song. (Romans 9-11 uses this kind of style too.) As we study them we shall come to realize that each chorus touches upon a definite matter—each expressing an important doctrine, ranging in subject matter from salvation to rapture. For the Holy Spirit to adopt in these eight passages the form of song to present these doctrines conveys the fact that there must be something of tremendous significance here.

Plan 21 Prayers

Prayers such as Abraham's prayer for Sodom and Gomorrah, Moses' prayer for rebellious Israel, David's prayers in the Psalms, the prayer in Ezra 9, in Nehemiah 9, in Daniel 9, the prayer which the Lord teaches His disciples in Matthew 6, His prayer in John 17, Paul's prayers in the Letter to the Ephesians: all of these need to be accurately studied one by one. By so doing we will solve many problems pertaining to prayer. We will then know what words should be uttered before God to be heard of Him. The words of the mouth as well as the thoughts of the heart are of great consequence in God's presence. The Lord Jesus said to the Syrophoenician woman, "*For this saying* go thy way; the demon is gone out of thy daughter" (Mark 7.29). This reveals how important indeed is the word employed in prayer.

Prayer sometimes fails because of unsuitable words. Often we come to God with many words without there being any result, until finally a particular word or two expressed seems to utter our need and then our prayer is heard. Once a brother had pleurisy. A number of brothers and sisters were concerned about his situation. They prayed for him. Many words were uttered but all were of no avail. Finally one sister prayed, and she used one word—"For in death there is no remembrance of thee: in Sheol who shall give thee thanks?" (Ps. 6.5)—and this word got through. That very afternoon that brother got out of bed. Hence, answered prayer and word are closely related. If the right word comes forth there will be miracle. Let us learn the way of prayer.

Plan 22   Bible Difficulties

To solve Bible difficulties several basic rules must be observed.

First, we must at the outset believe that the Bible itself has no difficulty. If there is any problem, it is due to *our* misunderstanding.

Second, we must not try to solve a Bible difficulty by only the local passage in question, for no Scripture is to be interpreted privately, that is, according to the local meaning by itself. Whenever a difficulty is encountered, study it with other Scripture passages before a judgment is made. Those difficult passages can never be in conflict with the teachings found in other passages of the Bible. In writing the Word, God does not forget what He has already written. If there seems to be any discrepancy it must be the fault of our own mentality.

Third, some words may not recur in other portions of the Scriptures. Even so, we ought to believe in them and never to disbelieve God's word through our own prejudice and reasonings.

Fourth, in order to solve a difficulty we must search for evidence. Find evidences both from the Scriptures and from reason. Whatever God has spoken is most certainly full of teaching, for He will never say any unreasonable thing.

Fifth, by difficulty is meant either a difficulty in interpretation of Scripture or a difficulty in the matter of a teaching. (We do not view as being a difficulty any discrepancy concerning numbers that appear in the Bible. Such number discrepancies are due to errors made in copying. During the period of the church's persecution, when Bibles were being destroyed, it was not an easy matter to make copies and so mistakes in copying were unavoidable. This, therefore, is not a problem involving inspiration. If anyone should use this to justify an attack on the Bible, his criticism is overblown.)

After we precisely understand the above rules, we may begin to collect all the apparent difficulties in the Bible. The following are examples: "the sons of God" in Genesis 6; "An old man cometh up . . . And Saul perceived that it was Samuel" in 1 Samuel 28.14; "knoweth no one . . . neither the Son" in Matthew 24.36; the "two swords" in Luke 22.38; "Whose soever sins ye forgive, they are forgiven unto them" in John 20.23; "It is impossible to renew them again unto repentance" in Hebrews 6.6; "There remaineth no more . . . sacrifice for sins" in Hebrews 10.26; "the spirits in prison" in 1 Peter 3.19; and, "the gospel preached even to the dead" in 1 Peter 4.6. All these may be taken as difficulties in interpreting the Scriptures. Others like "camel to go through a needle's eye" have been solved for four hundred years, and hence they cannot any longer be considered to be difficulties. Paul's going to Jerusalem in Acts 21 is not a difficulty in interpretation; rather, it is a difficulty in event.

Now as one example, let us attempt to solve an *Old* Testament difficulty according to the above rules.

"The sons of God" in Genesis 6 bears a significant relationship to the second coming of the Lord Jesus. For "as it came to pass in the days of Noah," said the Lord Jesus, "even so shall it be also in the days of the Son of man" (Luke 17.26). How were the days of Noah? The sons of God came in to the daughters of men. Many commentators interpret this affair as indicating that the sons of Seth married the daughters of Cain. But such an interpretation is forced. When "the sons of God" married the daughters of men, they bore the Nephilim (i.e., the giants; the original meaning of Nephilim is "the fallen"). How could the sons of Seth (by this interpretation being "the sons of God"), in marrying the daughters of Cain, father giants? Seth was a human being, and so was Cain. How could the same kind of human beings beget a different type of men? Such an interpretation is bound to convey an unnatural cast to the affair.

Who, then, are "the sons of God"? Naturally the answer must especially be sought in the Old Testament. By searching, the evidence appears. We can safely conclude that "the sons of God" here point to the angels. We find some strong evidence in the book of Job. Job was written before the book of Genesis, for the latter was compiled during the time of Moses whereas the former was composed at the time of Abraham. Such a dating of these two books has been commonly accepted. The words employed in later Biblical writings usually follow those of the earlier writings. In Job 1, 2 and 38, the phrase "the sons of God" refers in all cases to the angels; so that quite naturally "the sons of God" in Genesis 6 must likewise have reference to the angels.

The Lord Jesus noted that "in the resurrection they neither marry, nor are given in marriage, but are as angels in heaven" (Matt. 22.30). Yet this statement does not suggest that angels are not able to marry or to be given in marriage; the statement merely says that angels *do not* marry nor are given in marriage. God forbids the angels to marry for they are spirits. Nonetheless an unexpected thing happened; the most confusing of all things occurred in the time of Genesis 3, and that was that the Satanic spirit entered into a lower creature—the serpent. So that in Genesis we observe a union of the evil spirit with the lower creature. And in the time of Genesis 6 the evil spirit entered into a union with men. Angels ought not marry, nevertheless they married the daughters of men and begat the Nephilim. And when the Nephilim appeared on the earth, God decided to destroy them. God wants angels, He wants men, but He does not want the Nephilim; for He has not created such a species. All that He has made must be each after its kind. But out of the union of the devils and men came forth the Nephilim. God therefore severely judged them. Why, as a further example, did God decide to destroy the Anakim who appeared later on? Because they too were Nephilim. Originally the Nephilim were destroyed in the flood, but later in the land of Canaan the Nephilim appeared again in the form of the Anakim. They too must be destroyed. For God will not allow such kind of creature to exist on the earth.

The passage in Jude 6—"And angels that kept not their own principality, but left their proper habitation"—likewise refers to the marriage of the angels. Also, "angels when they sinned" (2 Peter 2.4) points to the same affair.

The passage in Genesis 6.3 is clear: "for that he [man] also is flesh." What is meant here by the word "also"? It means the second time. For instance, You have eaten, but I also have eaten. This "also" means the second time. God says that man also is flesh, indicating that before man somebody else has first become flesh. Who, aside from man, can be spoken in such parallel fashion to man? None but the angel. Hence in saying that man *also* is flesh, it implies that the angels had already become flesh. With such evidence as this, we can assuredly conclude that "the sons of God" point to the angels.

Man indeed had sinned in Genesis 3, but the sinning in Genesis 3 and the becoming flesh in Genesis 6 are not the same. To sin is a matter of conduct, not a matter of nature; but to become flesh signifies that the whole being is now controlled by the flesh; so that it has become a matter of nature. We must pay attention to the subsequent development of man's sin besides the original fall of man recorded in Genesis 3. For Adam it is a sinful act, for Cain it has become a lust, and by the time of the flood, sin has developed so quickly that man has become flesh; that is, sinning has now become a habit. Ever since man had first sinned, the Spirit of God had always striven with him until he became flesh. The words, "My Spirit shall not strive with man for ever", show that from the Garden of Eden until the flood the Spirit of God had been striving with man. Yet when man became so licentious as to become flesh, God's Spirit ceased to strive any longer.

Why should we notice this matter? Because the Bible has declared: "And as were the days of Noah, so shall be the coming of the Son of man" (Matt. 24.37). This problem must therefore be solved. It is possible that before the coming of the Son of man the evil spirit of Satan will come to the earth, and sinful angels will at that time clothe themselves with flesh. These "sons of God" are always a problem; consequently God must judge them severely. The judgment of the flood is without precedent; the judgment of the land of Canaan is also exceedingly stern;

and at the coming of the Son of man there will come a great judgment. The Lord will judge the angels who fail to keep their original state.

Are those angels who have left their original state included in the third part (see Rev. 12.4) or not? Probably they are outside the third part of the angelic hosts who rebelled. "And angels that kept not their own principality, but left their proper habitation" (Jude 6). The word "principality" is translated by Darby as "original state". It means more than a *position,* it also signifies an original *condition.* The original condition of angels is neither marrying nor giving in marriage. To say "kept not their original state" means to say that they lost it through marriage. "Original state" refers to their condition, while "habitation" points to their dwelling. What has happened to these angels? Jude 6 continues with: "He [the Lord] hath kept [them] in everlasting bonds under darkness unto the judgment of the great day." Now the first word— "even"—in verse 7 is not to be found in the original Greek text, for verse 7 and verse 6 do not refer to two different matters; rather, verse 7 explains verse 6. Both J. N. Darby's translation and Stephen's text of 1550 omit the word "even". For these angels, just "as Sodom and Gomorrah and the cities about them, having in like manner with these giving themselves over to fornication and gone after strange flesh, are set forth as an example, suffering the punishment of eternal fire" (v.7). This refers not to the fornication of the people of Sodom and Gomorrah, but to the angels, who—like the inhabitants of Sodom and Gomorrah—committed fornication and went after strange flesh. In other words, these angels did nothing but fornication. They forgot everything, and only indulged in fornication. They went after strange flesh, and so they were "set forth as an example, suffering the punishment of eternal fire." We may therefore say that Jude 6-7 explains Genesis 6.

Let us now illustrate our point a second time, but with a *New* Testament difficulty.

"Whose soever sins ye forgive, they are forgiven unto them" (John 20.23). This is in truth a most difficult problem. How can men have the authority to forgive? On the basis of this Scripture verse, the Roman Church formerly sold the so-called "indulgences". Actually, though, this verse is clearly related to the preceding verse, which reads: "Receive ye the Holy Spirit." In other words, the Lord gives His Holy Spirit to His church that she may represent Him on earth and be His vessel to forgive sins.

Such forgiveness we may label as "borrowed forgiveness". For instance, when we are preaching the gospel we sometimes meet a sinner who truly acknowledges himself to be a sinner and sincerely asks God for forgiveness with cries, tears, repentance, and faith in the Lord Jesus; but somehow he is unfamiliar with the truth of forgiveness. If at that moment someone in the church will stand up and say, "God has forgiven your sins", such a declaration will be of tremendous help to that sinner. The reason the church may decide who can be baptized and who can partake in the breaking of bread is because she has received the Holy Spirit. Under the authority of the Holy Spirit, she may be a borrowed hand to forgive or to retain people's sins. It is only when the church *abides in the Holy Spirit,* and breathes in the Holy Spirit that she can forgive. Not anyone can forgive merely on the ground of some fleshy position he occupies. If we can see such forgiveness as "borrowed forgiveness", the difficulty is solved.

The above are just two examples of Bible difficulty. In

explaining a Bible difficulty, we must gather sufficiently clear evidences, observe the context carefully, never interpret arbitrarily, nor follow any preconceived idea.

Plan 23 Book by Book

We may also study the Bible book by book. Read the Pentateuch, the Histories, the Psalms and the Prophets. Try to remember the contents of each book. In studying the Prophets, clearly distinguish the prophets before captivity, during captivity, and after captivity. While studying the New Testament, notice what the historical books, the epistles, the personal letters, and the prophecy say respectively. Each child of God may not be able to interpret every book in the Bible, but he should at least know what they are talking about. We need to spend two years at the very least to get a general idea of the sixty-six books of the Bible. If we wish to be even more acquainted with them, we may have to spend five or six years on them. Being well acquainted with the contents of each book, we are then able to make cross references between them as well as to know the nature of each of these books. And when we are studying the Old Testament, we can relate its books to those of the New Testament such as Romans, Ephesians, and Colossians. This too is a basic learning which should not be neglected.

Plan 24 Intimate Knowledge of a Few Books

After we finish studying the general outline of the whole Bible, we next should select a few books in which to make a special study. These books need to be studied carefully.

In the Old Testament we should study at least Genesis, Daniel, and Song of Solomon. If possible, add one more book from the Pentateuch—either Exodus, Numbers, or Leviticus. As regards the prophetic books, perhaps add Zechariah. Even though Isaiah has its peculiar value, many of its prophecies have already been fulfilled. Zechariah, as does Daniel, has many passages still waiting to be fulfilled. For this reason, we choose Zechariah.

In the New Testament we should study Matthew, Romans, Ephesians, and Revelation as a minimum; for these four books give basic teaching. If there is time, perhaps study also John and 2 Corinthians. After mastering these five or six books, the others can be added gradually. And thus shall we be able to be intimately acquainted with ten to twenty books after a decade or two.

Plan 25 Christ

Many tell us that the Bible speaks exclusively of Christ. The purpose of the entire Bible is to enable people to know Him. From the Old Testament to the New, there is a line showing us consistently who Christ is. We can find Christ in Genesis 1. Verse 26 reveals the consultation within the Godhead concerning the creation of man. And the very next verse reads: "And God created man in his own image, in the image of God created he him; male and female created he them." According to grammar, if verse 26 uses "us", verse 27 should use "they"; but we find "he" instead. This plainly indicates that the "he" here is Christ, because in the Godhead only Christ possesses a likeness. So that in the actual creation, man is made according to His likeness.

Genesis 3 mentions the seed of the woman. Matthew 1

shows us that the son of Mary is the seed of the woman. Reading on through Genesis, Exodus, Leviticus, Numbers, and Deuteronomy, we will discover these books to be full of Christ. In the life of David and within the pre-Captivity prophetic books such as Isaiah and Jonah, they too are full of Christ. Prophetic writings during the Captivity such as Jeremiah, Ezekiel, and Daniel and post-Captivity prophetic records like Haggai, Zechariah, and Malachi are likewise full of Christ.

We may see Christ not only in prophecy but also in the many rituals. First, there are the offerings in Genesis and Leviticus. Offerings continue after the building of the temple. In these offerings and sacrifices, we may see Christ. Second, in the cleansing of the leper, in the purification with the ashes of the red heifer, and in the washings of the priests, we may also see Christ. Third, in the priestly ministry as well as in the priestly garment we may again see Christ. And fourth, in the various feasts we may once more see Christ.

Many persons serve as types of Christ. Such types are of two kinds: one is expressed and the other is coincident. What are expressed types? "Behold, a greater than Solomon is here" (Luke 11.31), declares the Lord Jesus. This shows that Solomon is a type of Christ. Again, "For as Jonah was three days and three nights in the belly of the whale; so shall the Son of man be three days and three nights in the heart of the earth" (Matt. 12.40). This plainly states that Jonah too stands as a type of Christ. Furthermore, Galatians 3 tells us that Isaac also is a type of Christ. What are coincident types? Joseph, for instance, is not an expressed type. Though his experience is similar to Christ's in many points, nowhere in the whole Bible is Joseph clearly mentioned as a type of Christ. Accordingly, there are people who are expressly said to be types of

Christ, and there are other people who are like Christ but are considered as coincident types. Adam, Noah, Joseph, David, or Jehoshaphat all belong to this kind of type.

Besides persons there are other types such as manna, the brazen serpent, the tabernacle, Jacob's ladder, and so forth. All these objects are types of Christ. The Old Testament sometimes uses two birds, sometimes two kings, sometimes two priests, and sometimes two guides to typify Christ. In the case of the two birds—one represents death, the other represents resurrection; with the two kings—one represents war, the other represents peace; concerning the two priests—one stands for the earthly, Aaron, the other stands for the heavenly, Melchizedek; and as to the two guides—one leads out of Egypt, the other leads into Canaan. All these types speak of Christ.

When we come to the New Testament we see in the Gospels the history of Christ, His teaching, His miracles, and His prophecies. In the Acts we learn how He reigns today. In the Epistles we see how He dwells in man. It is a very good training indeed to uncover this line concerning Christ that runs from Genesis to Revelation.

Plan 26 Terminology

This kind of study is as comprehensive as it is important. We have mentioned before about topical study. Terminological study bears a certain resemblance to topical study, though they are actually different. In topical study, a topic that is not necessarily a term in the Bible is chosen and studied according to its spirit as well as to its content. Gathering all places in God's word which are similar both in spirit and in substance, and studying them, is called topical study. To study a term, however, is to discover all the places where the same word is used and make a study of them. In such a study we may use a concordance as we search the Scriptures.

The following are a few examples of terms we may study: sin, death, repentance, faith, forgiveness, reconciliation, mercy, grace, righteousness, law, law as principle, life, work, old, new, crucified, blood, save, redemption, substitute, raise (meaning to revive), son, priest, offerings, holy, love, hope, heart, spirit, light, joy, peace, truth, glory, prayer, blessing, promise, comfort, food, obedience, suffering, temptation, world, flesh, natural, anger, mind, dispensation, all, mountain. We may multiply this number three or four times, but the above items should be enough for the beginner. Such study will help us to understand the meaning of these terms as well as to know how many times these words are used. By setting these principal terms in order, we may comprehend what God intends to say through them.

Take the word "joy" for example. Find out all the Scripture verses on joy, write down especially those with any teaching concerning this subject, and arrange them in proper order—such as, When should we rejoice? Where comes our joy? What kind of person cannot be joyful? How can we be joyful? Thus shall we come to understand "joy".

Or, take another word in the Bible—"food". Let us search out all the places where the word or idea of food is used. We find in John 4.34: "My meat [or food] is to do the will of him that sent me, and to accomplish his work"; in Psalm 37.3: "Feed on his faithfulness"; and in Numbers 14.9: "Neither fear ye the people of the land; for they are bread [or food] for us". This last instance was spoken by Joshua and Caleb after the ten spies had given an evil report, saying: "The land through which we have gone to spy it out, is a land that eateth up the inhabitants thereof;

and all the' people that we saw in it are men of great stature. . . . And we were in our own sight as grasshoppers" (Num. 13.32,33).

Put these three places together and we see three different kinds of food: First, to do the Father's will is food. All who do the will of the Father grow stronger because they have food to eat. Due to hunger, the Lord Jesus sent His disciples into the city of Samaria to buy food; yet when they came back with it the Lord said, "I have meat to eat." The disciples therefore said to one another, "Hath any man brought him aught to eat?" To which the Lord replied, "My meat is to do the will of him that sent me, and to accomplish his work" (John 4.32-34). This shows us that far from work weakening us, it should strengthen us. Not only prayer can satisfy us, work can also fill us full. If we serve God well in the field as did our Lord we should naturally feel fed, since doing the Father's will is our food. Second, the Lord's faithfulness is our food. God is a God of faithfulness. We may feed on His faithfulness. Time and again God hears our prayers, and so we are becoming stronger all the time. Each time we trust God to carry us through we become fuller than before. The more we trust in Him the more satisfied we are and the stronger we become. For the faithfulness of the Lord is our food. Third, the "Nephilim" is also our food. With each giant we devour we grow a little stronger. If we eat one today, we may eat two tomorrow, and four the day after tomorrow. And with each occasion we become increasingly satisfied and stronger. Many are weak because they have not overcome the Nephilim in Canaan land. In other words, whatever trial or tribulation comes our way is God-given food for us. If we are unable to eat it, we shall feel hungry; but if we devour it, we will become strong and the tribulation is over.

One brother did some study once on the word "calling" or "God's calling". He quoted a number of Scriptures and divided the subject into ten parts. Let us list them for our reference.

Part 1   The source of calling
  1   Original source—God (1 Thess. 2.12)
  2   Mediate source—Jesus Christ (Rom. 1.6)

Part 2   The called
  1   Scope: general—all people (1 Cor. 1.24)
  2   Scope: spiritual—sinners (Luke 5.32)
  3   God's estimate—vessels of mercy (Rom. 9.23,24)
  4   Actual fact—not many wise (1 Cor. 1.26)

Part 3   The purpose of calling
  1   Repentance (Luke 5.32)
  2   Salvation (2 Thess. 2.13,14)
  3   Peace (Col. 3.15)
  4   Light (1 Peter 2.9)
  5   Fellowship (1 Cor. 1.9)
  6   Service (Rom. 1.1)
  7   Liberty (Gal. 5.13)
  8   Sanctification (1 Cor. 1.2)
  9   Suffering (1 Peter 2.21)
 10   Eternal life (1 Tim. 6.12)
 11   Eternal inheritance (Heb. 9.15)
 12   Eternal glory (1 Peter 5.10)

Part 4   The principles of calling
  1   According to God's purpose (Rom. 8.28)
  2   According to God's grace (2 Tim. 1.9)
  3   Not according to man's work (2 Tim. 1.9)

Part 5   The sphere of calling
  1   In the Lord (1 Cor. 7.22)
  2   In grace (Gal. 1.6)
  3   In peace (1 Cor. 7.15)
  4   In sanctification (1 Thess. 4.7)
  5   In the body (Col. 3.15)

Part 6   The ways of calling
  1   Through the gospel (2 Thess. 2.14)
  2   Through God's grace (Gal. 1.15)
  3   Through God's glory (2 Peter 1.3)
  4   Through God's virtue (2 Peter 1.3)

Part 7   The nature of calling
  1   Holy (2 Tim. 1.9)
  2   High (Phil. 3.14)
  3   Heavenly (Heb. 3.1)
  4   Humble (1 Cor. 1.26)

Part 8   The demand of calling
  1   Abide in the calling (1 Cor. 7.20,24)
  2   Walk in the calling (1 Cor. 7.17)
  3   Worthily of the calling (Eph. 4.1)
  4   Walk worthily of God (1 Thess. 2.12)
  5   Give more diligence (2 Peter 1.10)

Part 9   The encouragement of calling
  1   Hope of calling (Eph. 1.18, 4.4)
  2   Prize of calling (Phil. 3.14)

Part 10   The guarantee of calling
  1   God's nature—faithfulness (1 Cor. 1.9; 1 Thess. 5.24)
  2   God's plan (Rom. 11.29)
  3   God's grace (Rom. 8.30)

In all these Scripture verses the term "calling" can be found. By classifying these verses into the above ten parts a person is able to obtain quite a good understanding of the things relating to calling. If anyone can study a few dozen of these terms, he will gain some foundation in the knowledge of the Bible.

Turning now to other examples of terms we can look into, the word "generation" can be frequently observed as we study Genesis, such as in 5.1: "This is the book of the generations of Adam." In studying Exodus pay attention to the "ordinance" of the Lord. In Leviticus the word "holy" is frequently used. In Psalms such words as "My word", "adversary", "wait", and "Selah" are often seen. In Proverbs we encounter words like "wisdom", "lie", "wicked", "slothful", "proud", "heart", "tongue", "lips", "eye", etc. In Ecclesiastes the most frequently used words are "vanity" and "under the sun". In Song of Solomon words such as "love" and "myrrh" recur. In Matthew note "righteousness" and "the kingdom of the heavens", terms which occur often. There are at least eight times in Matthew when the Lord is seen on the mountain (4.8, 5.1, 14.23, 15.29, 17.1, 24.3, 26.30). On each occasion something happens. In Mark notice the word "straightway". In Luke observe the term "the Son of man". In John one should note such words as "sent", "world", "Father", and "abide". In Acts look for the word "Spirit". In Romans examine the words "death", "faith", and "righteousness". In Galatians the word "love" is rarely used and the word "holy" is never seen. In Ephesians, however, "love" and "holy" are used often. All these things must be discerned and none carelessly overlooked.

Sometimes in a passage or several passages of the Scriptures the same word is used many times. For instance, in 1 Chronicles 16 and Psalm 71 the word "continually" is used seven times (1 Chron. 16.6,11 AV, 37,40; Ps. 71.3,6,14). In Psalm 86 the word "for" is found on eight occasions. In Joshua 23 the phrase "Jehovah your God" is mentioned thirteen times. Ezra 7 records seven things of God (the hand of Jehovah, the law of Jehovah, the house of Jehovah, the will of God, the altar of the house of Jehovah, the servants of the house of God, and the wisdom of God). Paul in his epistles refers several times to "whatsoever ye do"—"Whatsoever ye do, . . . do all in the name of the Lord Jesus", "Whatsoever ye do, work heartily", and "Whatsoever ye do, do all to the glory of God" (Col. 3.17,23; 1 Cor. 10.31). The Gospel of John and his epistles mention "joy . . . made full" six times (John 3.29, 15.11, 16.24, 17.13; 1 John 1.4; 2 John 12). No less than five times does Paul intersperse his letters with either "thank God" or "thanks be to God" (Rom. 6.17, 7.25; 1 Cor. 15.57; 2 Cor. 2.14, 9.15). The terms "victory" in Revelation, "precious" in Peter and "joy" in Philippians have their respective purpose and meaning. In our reading the Bible these distinctive terms should be studied and outlined. Such study is highly profitable to us.

Plan 27 Doctrine

The Bible contains seven basic doctrines: the doctrine of God the Father, the Son of God, the Holy Spirit, sin, redemption, Christian life and living, and the future. These are cardinal doctrines in theology.

Concerning God the Father, we should ferret out and collect all the Bible verses pertaining to God's name, God's heart, His nature, His virtue, His power, His authority, the relation between the Father and the Son, how God redeems, and so forth.

While He was on earth the Lord Jesus himself said that He is the Son. Hence the Lord Jesus is eternally the Son. Yet the declaration concerning the Son is made in the Bible in the context of reference to the resurrection. For the verse in Hebrews 1.5—"this day have I begotten thee"—points to the resurrection of our Lord. So also does Romans 1.4 speak of the same thing: "declared to be the Son of God . . . by the resurrection from the dead."

After completing a study of the doctrines concerning the Father and the Son, we may next consider the doctrine of the Holy Spirit. To know the Holy Spirit we should at least understand His work both outside of man and inside of man. These two works need to be distinguished, otherwise there is no possibility of a clear knowledge of the Holy Spirit.

We may then study the problems of sin, of redemption, of the daily living of God's children, and of the future. Delve into them one by one. Theology deals mostly with these seven matters. We will have a firm grasp of basic doctrines if we possess a clear understanding of these seven.

Plan 28   Progress of Doctrine

All who read the Bible come to recognize one thing: that the Bible is God's revelation given us by diverse portions and in diverse manners (see Heb. 1.1). God not only gives His revelation in diverse manners but also through diverse portions, and each revelation of God advances a little further beyond the preceding one. We should learn from the Scriptures how divine doctrine makes its progress. This does not imply that the revelation of the Bible is not complete, for the revelation of God throughout the whole Bible is perfect and complete. Even so, God's revelation is progressive in its unveiling. God has His revelation at the first stage, but then He adds more revelation at the second stage, even more at the third stage, and so on until it is full and complete. His revelation at any such stage cannot be considered as incomplete; yet in comparison to the total revelation it appears to be partial. Take for instance God's revelation to Abraham. During the time of Abraham, it was complete. But considering it from the viewpoint of the full revelation we have today, we must feel the revelation at Abraham's time to be insufficient. We must therefore learn to see how God's revelation comes from Adam, from Noah, from Abraham, from Israel, from Moses, and so forth. For the revelation of God progresses all the time.

We need also to learn how to distinguish God's dispensational truth from God's eternal truth. Some truths in the Bible are meant for a particular dispensation, while others are for eternal use. Sometimes God gives a command in a certain period, but that command is not designed for permanent application. For example, God commanded the children of Israel to destroy the Canaanites. This is a dispensational truth, not an eternal one. It is therefore extremely important for us to discern eternal truth as well as dispensational truth. Some words are dispensational words, spoken to the people of that time but not to all people at all times. Some words are eternal words, for they are spoken to people in latter times as well as to those people hearing them when first spoken. In studying the Bible we need to discover what are dispensational truths and what are eternal truths, which were for a particular period and which are to be continued on into eternity. These two kinds of truths should be clearly distinguished, or else many difficulties in the Word cannot be solved.

Many have the erroneous idea of thinking that all the words of the Old Testament are spoken only to the people of the Old Testament; and thus they make the whole of the Old Testament dispensational truth. Many others have the equally mistaken concept of viewing all the words in the Old Testament as being words spoken to us, thereby making the entire Old Testament eternal truth. However, we should separate dispensational truth from eternal truth. When God speaks to people of a certain period, if it is for contemporary use we call it dispensational truth. But if it is to be applied to people of all times we call it eternal truth. Eternal truth is progressive in character: at one period God speaks a few words, and then at another period He adds on more words. But there is one thing we should always keep well in mind; which is, that the progression of truth is confined within the scope or framework of the Bible. Any teaching outside of the Scriptures cannot be considered as progress of truth. In Genesis we see God as the Creator, Ruler, Law-giver, Judge, and Redeemer. These five aspects of the truth of God are gradually developed throughout the whole Old Testament. In the same book of Genesis we also see that the creation of man is glorious, the fall of man is shameful, that man needs salvation, that he seeks after God, and that he tries to be saved by works. And once again, these five points concerning the doctrine of man are fully developed in the entire New Testament. Such we call the progress of doctrine.

From Adam to Samuel we see "God's rule", for God rules directly over His own people. From David, Solomon and onward to the Babylonian captivity, we see the "kings' rule", since God rules His people through the kings. Beginning with the return from the Babylonian captivity and running until the Lord Jesus, we see the "prophets' and priests' rule." Thus the line is from "God's rule" to "kings' rule" to "prophets' and priests' rule", from the beginning to the end, a movement from outside control to inside control. The outward has failed, but "righteousness" has come inside. This doctrine is also progressive.

Coming to the New Testament, the four Gospels speak distinctly of Christ in an ever progressive manner. We may view the four Gospels in seven stages.

1) The Lord Jesus is proving himself to be the Messiah. This unfolds itself in Jerusalem, Judea, and Samaria and is the situation found in John 1-4.

2) After the Messiahship is proven, the problem of the kingdom of the heavens arises. So then, Matthew 4 declares the kingdom, Chapters 5-7 describe the contents of the kingdom, and Chapter 13 deliberates the mysteries of the kingdom. Thus does the second stage make advance through the problem of the kingdom.

3) The stage which proves the Person of the Son of God commences with the Lord's multiplication of the loaves to feed the five thousand. This event is especially narrated in the Gospel according to John. Although the other Gospels record the same incident, the narrative of John carries with it a special implication. He points out particularly that this incident proves Jesus Christ to be the Son of God. And following this comes Peter's confession in Caesarea that the Lord is the Christ, the Son of the living God. Then occurs the transfiguration of the Lord on the mount. All these are recorded to prove the Person of the Lord Jesus.

4) Coming down from the Mount of Transfiguration, Jesus sets His face towards Jerusalem. For this Christ is to suffer and to die (see Matt. 16.21; Luke 9.31).

5) Upon entering Jerusalem the Lord Jesus speaks of

His second coming, which is followed up by the prophecies He utters on the Mount of Olives (see Matt. 24,25).

6) On the evening of the Passover the Lord Jesus
speaks to His disciples in a room about the coming of the
Holy Spirit, the parable of the vine, and so forth (see John
14-17).

7) The risen Christ commissions His disciples to
preach the gospel.

By a study of the Gospels in which we set forth as
seven mountain peaks these seven stages of the history of
Christ, we can clearly comprehend the entire life story of
the Lord Jesus.

When we come to Acts three matters are of special
significance: 1) the resurrection of the Lord Jesus, 2) the
rule and reign of the Lord Jesus, and 3) the forgiveness
given by the Lord Jesus. In other words, a risen Lord is
reigning today, and His gospel of forgiveness is to be
preached to all people at the same time. Consequently, we
can plainly detect a progress in Acts that is beyond the
Gospels.

Then come the epistles of Paul. Let us notice his
writings in the Bible and their chronological order. He first
writes 1 Thessalonians, then 2 Thessalonians, followed in
order by 1 Corinthians, 2 Corinthians, Galatians, Romans,
Philemon, Colossians, Ephesians, Philippians, 1 Timothy,
Titus, and lastly 2 Timothy (If Hebrews is reckoned as
written by Paul, it should be placed before 1 Timothy). All
his writings may be divided into four categories: (1) 1 and
2 Thessalonians speak on the second coming of the Lord;
(2) 1 and 2 Corinthians and Galatians correct the errors of
the believers; (3) Romans, Philemon, Colossians, Ephesians and Philippians declare Christ; and (4) 1 Timothy,
Titus, and 2 Timothy deal with the government and order
and like-problems of the church: they do not add to

revelation because the revelation God gives to Paul has reached its summit in Ephesians.

It is therefore evident that the doctrines in the Bible steadily advance. At the time of Paul the problem of the church is completely solved, the errors of the believers are fully corrected, the riches of the church are manifested, and the second coming of Christ is proclaimed. This we call progress. As to the books of Hebrews, James, 1 and 2 Peter, and Jude, they belong to a different class, possess their peculiar features, and are commonly known as "the catholic epistles". Hebrews shows us the New Covenant; James, works; 1 and 2 Peter, suffering and hope; and Jude, the preservation of faith. These letters are written to solve fragmentary problems of Christians. They do not advance the revelation. And finally, there are the epistles of John and John's revelation. And here is another advance—this one made by John. For Paul gives us truth, but John gives us theology. John shows us especially the reality of Christianity which is God's life. Both his epistles and revelation bring us to God.

Hence all the truths in the Bible are in a state of progress, with each truth advancing to its peak. There is revelation in one book, added revelation in another book, and so on and so forth, until it comes to one book where the revelation reaches its peak. Let us use "righteousness" as an example. Notice how righteousness commences in Matthew until it arrives at its peak in Romans and Galatians. Or take the matter of "the church"—it begins at Matthew 16 and climbs step by step till it is fully resolved in Ephesians. Or take the example of "life"—it commences with the Gospel of John and advances and peaks in the epistles of John.

Study the Bible book by book, noting how each problem begins, where is there some addition, and finally in which book it is thoroughly resolved. And interestingly enough, once a problem is solved in a certain book, this problem is no longer mentioned in the latter writings. There must be a book which solves one or more problems; but afterwards, these problems are either left unmentioned or are only casually referred to. There is no more new revelation. Upon completion of the writing of the whole Bible, the revelations of God have all reached their peaks. God's revelation increases and advances until the entire Bible is finished, and then the highest perfection is arrived at.

Accordingly, in studying the Scriptures we must do two things. First, find out where revelation is in the Bible—that is, where does a revelation commence. And second, find out where any new thoughts or any new revelations are being added. Search step by step and make notes. In which book is there a beginning, in which book is there a new explanation, in which book is there any new revelation. Whether it is a new explanation or a new revelation, collect and arrange according to order. After gathering all the revelations and explanations, analyze them carefully so as to come to a judgment concerning a particular truth. This is theology. Orthodox theology is a discovery of the truths of the Scriptures. And such study will give us a clear understanding of Bible truths.

We terminate the methods of Bible study here.

To conclude the whole matter, then, let us reiterate that the *man* must be right; otherwise, even if we have worked with all twenty-eight methods of studying the Bible we are not profited, because "the letter killeth, but the spirit giveth life" (2 Cor. 3.6). We do not suggest that the man has to be fully prepared before he can read the

Scriptures; we simply affirm that in the study of the Word we must pay attention to man's condition before God. If we are to reap an abundant harvest and to obtain a rich supply, we must on the one side have a right condition before God and on the other side spend time in practicing the methods of Bible study.

TITLES YOU
WILL WANT TO HAVE

by Watchman Nee

by Stephen Kaung

ORDER FROM:

Christian Fellowship Publishers, Inc.

Box 58

Hollis, New York 11423